ALSO BY BILL LIGHTLE

Made or Broken: Football & Survival in the Georgia Woods

12/17/09

To Mr. L.M. "Doc" Bridges,

Best Wishes

MILL DADDY
The Life & Times of Roy Davis

Bill Lightle

BILL LIGHTLE

Mill City Press, Inc.
212 3rd Avenue North, Suite 290
Minneapolis, MN 55401
612.455.2294
www.millcitypublishing.com

ISBN - 978-1-936107-26-1
ISBN - 1-936107-26-0
LCCN - 2009936591

Cover Design by Alan Pranke
Typeset by James Arneson

Printed in the United States of America

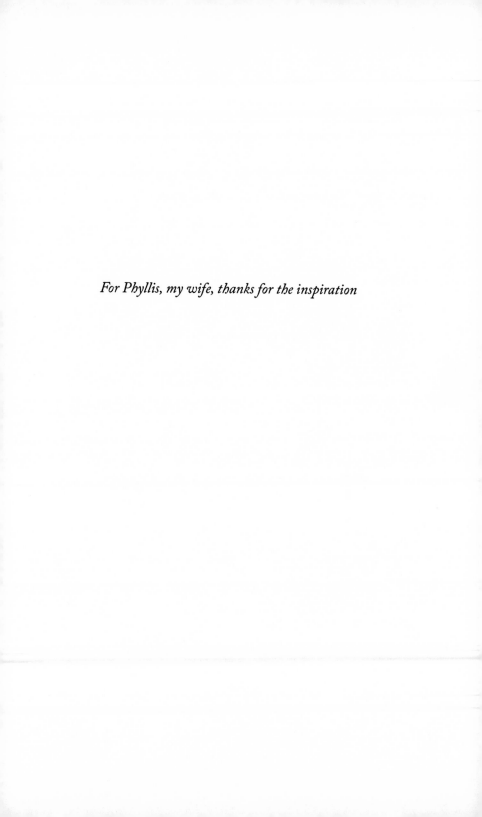

For Phyllis, my wife, thanks for the inspiration

INTRODUCTION

Roy Davis' life from our distance today was one of punishing work that was not honored by those who profited from it. From any distance it was one of everlasting spirit whose laughter and love arose from the hardscrabble fields on which he came of age. He had been a cotton picker, a mill hand, and a military man. To me he was an authentic American hero.

Roy was born not long into the last century and into a sharecropping family in Baker County, Georgia. From there Roy moved to the village at the Flint River Cotton Mill in Albany in the 1930s. And there he met Anna Carnes, a pretty mill girl from Crisp County, Georgia, fell in love with her, married her, reared children together, and they remained devoted to one another into the next century.

I met Roy in the early 1970s along with some of my high school friends working under him on Sundays, cleaning the mill's air conditioning system as it was shut down for production. Roy called himself a "humidity man" having worked in maintenance most of his mill life.

This story is about Roy's working and family life and the times my friends and I spent at the mill, sometimes working and sometimes playing. Now that my "lint head brothers" are into our 50s, we still talk of Roy and fondly remember our days at the mill with him.

I interviewed Roy and Anna and other family members a few years ago, and I'm grateful for their time and the stories they shared with me. By then Roy and Anna's health and memories were both declining some. But they did as best they could in remembering and in telling their stories of heartache and hope.

Throughout the last part of this book I frequently use the phrase "lint heads" in describing myself and my friends who worked under Roy. I'm aware that years ago mill owners used that phrase as a pejorative in describing those who were making them wealthy. But we used that phrase at the mill in the 1970s, as I do in the book, in a light-hearted and non-demeaning manner. We were teenage boys having fun.

Thanks to my wife Phyllis for reading the manuscript and suggesting needed changes that I made. Some members of her Alabama family were mill hands, like many others years ago, and their stories and Roy's are woven with the same cotton fabric.

Bill Lightle
Albany, Georgia
August 2009

ONE

Roy Davis was hanging out with some tough poor boys at the mill village when he saw the girl with brown hair and eyes like diamonds in the faraway Georgia sky. He was in his 20s and not long out of the unforgiving piney woods and hard, red fields of Baker County, and into the mill. Anna Carnes was 14. By 15 everybody in the mill village knew she was Roy's girl.

She appeared that day when he first saw her as an "angel," Roy said. Anna was small, brittle, and often tired from the hard, hard life at the Flint River Cotton Mill. Most days she was a worn-out angel.

"She wasn't as big as a sack," Roy Davis said. "The wind could blow her down."

For Roy Davis a hurricane couldn't blow his short, stocky, hard-working body down and keep him away from Anna Carnes. After they had met, he became jealous of other mill boys who came "a-courtin'" his angel. He carried a .38 caliber pistol in his ragged pants pocket to "scare the hell" out of them. He never shot anyone over Anna but said he was willing to do so.

You'd believe him if you ever heard him tell it.

Anna thought Roy was just "another guy hangin' out," some days causing trouble, some days not. Anna's mother, Lou Cindy "Lucy" Carnes, didn't want her daughter seeing Roy. He was too old for the young and uncertain Anna.

Roy often called on Anna at her home in the village but her mother would chase him away from the front door. Roy would wait nearby for Lucy to leave the house or sometimes simply fall asleep exhausted from millwork, and then he would slip in the house through the back door. Once inside Roy helped Anna cook, wash clothes, and hang the clothes outside to dry in the hot, lint-thick air that could suffocate the village and the people in it.

Roy was stubborn, like a trapped possum, and determined to marry Anna despite her mother's objections. Roy's doggedness and the possibility that he might be able some day to give Anna something better than the life she had been living convinced her mother to "bless" the marriage.

"I didn't know he wanted to marry me," Anna said some sixty years later, still married to Roy.

She knew little about sex and what a wife should say and do married to an illiterate sharecropping boy who had become a mill-working man.

"I was so dumb and young," Anna said. "Momma didn't teach us nothin'."

Roy had captured his angel and would never let her fly away. On December 22, 1938, with the South and the rest of the country suffering through the Great Depression, Roy and Anna were married in Lee County, just north of Albany, by the justice of the peace. Six decades later they recalled little from their wedding day. Their best man's last name was "somethin' like Lockey," who was barefooted during the ceremony. Everything else about that day has faded into years of lost memory, both earthly and heavenly.

They have had five children, one who died in infancy, several grandchildren, a few great-grandchildren, foster children, and through 40 years of millwork at poverty pay, Roy has called Anna, "Momma." She has been his love force.

"I'd marry her every year if they'd let me," Roy said. A few times during their marriage they have renewed their wedding vows to "refresh" their love, as Roy tells it.

"I think we had a wonderful life…me and Momma."

Their hardships have been many.

•••••

Anna Carnes was born in 1923 in Crisp County, Georgia, about 40 miles east of Albany. She grew up on a farm, but her father, Les Carnes, had a steady job at a prison camp. It was regular money for those crying times.

Anna was about seven and had a younger sister, Rena, when her mother became pregnant. Before the new baby came, Les Carnes abandoned his family, taking with him another woman.

"We lived in an old hut by the sawmill. Daddy left us by the sawmill," Anna said.

With two children and another coming, Lucy Carnes cried into the night, frightened of what the future would be. Anna and Rena heard their mother cry, and they became scared. How was Lucy to feed and care for her children? Lucy had no education in a life and landscape already poor but made even poorer by the Great Depression. Women and children alone in this kind of world were confronted with hunger, maybe even starvation. The crying came easy.

Lucy gave birth to a boy and named him simply, C. H. The "C" was for Carnes and the "H" for Hardin, Lucy's maiden name. The name reflected the hope she had that her runaway husband would return and care again for his family.

"My mother thought my father would come back and name him," Anna Carnes said. "But he never did."

Hope never came and C. H. remained C. H. Lucy Carnes alone would have to find a way to provide for herself and her children. The shadow of hunger was growing.

With help from some relatives, Lucy moved her family to Albany into what Anna Carnes said was a wooden hut near present-day Chehaw State Park, a few miles east of downtown. Not long afterwards she found a job in the Flint River Cotton Mill and moved into a house in the mill village. She rented one room of the house while another mill family occupied the other room. This arrangement was common for Albany mill workers and others throughout the South. God might've wanted them to have a whole house but mill bosses would determine that.

The village was a clustering of simple company-owned redbrick and wooden houses with fireplaces for heat and cooking. There was no indoor plumbing. Mill families had outhouses and water pumps in their backyards. These houses were on today's Madison, Tenth, and Eleventh avenues.

"You weren't allowed to have a whole house," Anna said. Over the years her family would move three or four times within the village.

The best Anna could recollect was that her mother during the 1930s paid the company 25 cents a week to rent one room. Hanging from the ceiling was a single light bulb. At four each morning the company would allow the electricity to be used, but by 10 at night it was disengaged. The rhythms of work and light itself were cotton mill policy. Sometime in those early months in the village Anna's mother was able to convince the owners to move her family to a different house. It would have two rooms.

There was little time for school and play for Roy Davis' future wife.

"I learned how to cook on a fireplace," Anna said. "We had a pump in the backyard and I toted water."

At the mill Lucy Carnes earned about three to four dollars a week for working more than 40 hours. The work and the rearing of her children began to crush Lucy in the same mean way it was crushing women all over the South during the Great Depression.

"She stayed in bed most of the time when she wasn't workin'," Anna said. "Momma was sick a lot. The work was too hard for her, and I had to tend to the children." Her talk of sufferings long past evoked the memories of pain that the heart had not and will never completely purge.

Anna's mother did the best she could. She once asked the company, and it complied, to move her family from one mill house to another because the woman with whom they had been sharing the house had used profanity around her children. She always tried to protect the little ones.

Anna's sister, Rena, went to school but not her brother, C. H. The mill village included a school, store, and even a church. Lucy tried and tried to get C. H. in school.

"Momma would take him to school and he'd beat her back home," Anna said. "She whipped him all the way to the school-house, but it didn't do no good."

Lucy Carnes worked incessantly in the lint and the heat and the never-ending thunder noise of the mill where the cotton was woven into thread and cloth. But her children would only have life's raw necessities. Her relatives in Crisp County occasionally brought meat, vegetables, and syrup to Lucy and her children. The telling of this part of the story came with a cheek-to-cheek grin from Anna Carnes. It was the face of contentment that comes after a deed well done, or the look that a father has after his son has done some good and decent thing.

The Carnes children would have food in their bellies and clothes made from burlap sacks. Anna's mother carefully, patiently, and with tenderness that can accompany suffering made her children clothes with rough sacks, woven strong to carry many pounds.

"We had the prettiest clothes there ever was," Anna said.

Anna's family would eventually move near Roy Davis, who like haggard little Anna herself, had come to the mill village leaving behind the red fields of work and pain.

TWO

The crumbling wooden sharecropping shack still stood along a paved road that was built out of the clay, underbrush, and pine thickets of Baker County. This was where Roy was born about 30 miles south of Albany. On February 19, 1916, about one year before the United States entered World War I changing its relationship with the wider world, Roy came early upon this land. He called himself a seven-month baby.

This shack is near Elmodel, a spit of a settlement about ten miles from Newton, the county seat, just a bit bigger than a spit itself. Roy's house is rotten, leaning, and not long for this world. There were many like it on this land years ago but most have fallen or have been razed. All who had once lived in them had been poor, poor but not in spirit. They couldn't be. If their spirits had been impoverished, Roy's had not been, they would've died young. Roy's birth shack still stands. One day, too, it will fall.

Roy took me to his old home one Sunday morning in January 2002. There were spider webs thick as cotton fields, many empty tin cans and bottles, some decades old. The afternoon wind whipped through the holes in the walls echoing stories of love and despair. There was a large faded white-stone fireplace in the three-room house. Roy's mother cooked corn bread, bacon, and collard greens in that fireplace while her children huddled around it when the air turned cold those many years ago.

The day I was there it was gray and cloudy and only a passing vehicle, every few minutes over the smooth country road, reminded me that this was not the beginning of the last century. It was not the world that Roy had been born into. For a long way around the house, in all directions, there were tall Georgia pines bending slightly with the wind, but not breaking. Thickets and briars and tall brown grass moved too but still dead with winter. This land had changed little since Roy had walked on it as a boy.

Roy walked slowly around his old house with the help of a smooth-skinned walking cane. He wore a red sweater that was unbuttoned and a brown short-billed cap. A few weeks earlier he had undergone heart surgery and was wearing a pacemaker. The last five years Roy had been losing his eyesight. That day, and the days afterwards when I was with him, I held his arm to steady his walk.

"I can't see good more that ten feet," Roy said.

Roy could recall few detailed memories of living on the place where his life had begun. When he was young his father, Primus Davis, would move the family to similar sharecropping homes in the piney woods before his family moved to the mill village in Albany, next to Anna Carnes. Ollie Davis, Roy's mother, and Primus had seven children but one died in infancy and had to be consigned to the cold earth below. Ollie had miscarriages but no one in the family remembered how many. There could have been one or two, or four or five.

•••••

What is certain is that sharecropper's wives, like Ollie, had lots of children. In *Like a Family: The Making of a Southern Cotton Mill World*, published by the University of North Carolina Press, the author says that by the early 1900s southern farmwomen had the largest families in the country. After marrying, women usually had a baby every two years.

John Wesley Snipes was a southern sharecropping boy many years ago, the book said, and the fourth child his mother had in six years. "The babies came so fast," Snipes said, "that they were all the same size."

Vesta Finley was one of ten children and said that her mother "was mostly tied up with tending babies, having babies, and taking care of the home."

Ollie Davis was like other farmwomen of her era with no dependable birth control, unwilling to question her husband's sometime tyrannical authority and the acceptance of the wife's submissiveness in the bed, and in the bearing of children. The pines sway silently with the heartaches of dead farm mothers. And their relentless courage is found in the same music above.

●●●●●

Roy and I left his house, and I drove us down that country road across Nochaway Creek where as a dirt boy he swam in its brown waters and caught fish with his mother. We turned onto a dirt road thick with mud on both sides from the winter rains. A red-tail hawk flew out of an imposing oak tree, like a giant warrior overlooking a medieval castle. The beautiful raptor flew only ten feet above my car. Roy showed me other wooden shacks he had lived in and they began to stir his thoughts of being on this land, a little boy picking cotton, sometimes with bloody fingers but always doing a man's hard work.

Primus was a "good daddy," Roy said, "and he always seen that we had a little bit to eat." Roy's father had been a horse trader, sharecropper, and probably made and sold his own whiskey.

"He gave us a full tablespoon every night. Me and my brothers all had a snort," Roy said

Primus Davis, maybe from the whiskey money, eventually bought a piece of land himself in Baker County. He was, through Roy's memories, a "wheeler dealer" who often carried two .38 caliber pistols, one around his shoulder and the other on his hip. Primus made sure his boys worked the land and killed animals in the pine forest. He was a hard man who scared his own family, a man others might call an unforgiving son-of-a-bitch.

"Did he ever shoot anyone?" I said.

"I never knew of it if he did," Roy said.

One of Roy and Anna's own daughters, Bobbi Buffi, who was born in 1950 remembered her grandfather as a "mean man" who "horse whipped" his own children. Maybe he was part good as Roy said, but he had a monster hand of discipline.

"He'd beat the shit out of you with that bullwhip," Roy said.

When Roy was two or three, his older brother Robert shot Roy in the head with one of their father's guns. Primus and Ollie were away from the house when the accident happened. Roy rubbed his hand over the scarred wound as he told me the story. The bullet remained inside Roy's head. Lodged forever like the memories of work, sweat, and mean Primus himself.

"Robert was playin' cowboys and Injuns, but I wasn't, Daddy," Roy said. "Daddy" was the play name Roy used often referring to others. He called me that many times as well as my friends when we worked under Roy at the mill in the early 1970s.

Years after he shot Roy in the head, Robert was making illegal whiskey at a still near the cotton mill. Dead now for nearly 50 years, Robert liked the taste of whiskey himself. It had been a little-boy treat from his father. During the Great Depression Robert rode trains, jumping on and off and not paying, like thousands of others in this sad country who were looking for jobs, dignity or maybe trying to forget everything about that awful time. The family story is told that Robert fell off a train in Birmingham, Alabama, seriously injuring one of his legs. He could still be a hellcat though.

Not long after the accident, with Robert on crutches and living with Roy and his family at the mill village, the whiskey-drinking brother with only one good leg, shot and killed a man. Roy remembered the victim's name only as "Jacob" or "Jacobs." One of Roy's sisters, Agnes Moore, recalled the killing the same way as Roy.

Agnes was born in 1920, labored in the mill for nearly 30 years, and was a teenager when Robert killed that man. Many years have been swept away but her memory of that day remained sharp, like the whiskey her brother used to make.

"I saw it all," she said, some years ago from her house on Homewood Drive in Albany. "The man that Robert killed came to our house and asked Daddy to loan him 25 dollars."

That was nearly a month's wage for some mill workers in the 1930s. The man who wanted the money appeared drunk and Primus Davis, the father sometimes adorned with two .38 caliber pistols, chased him away from the house. But the money seeker didn't leave the property.

He hid outside of the house, maybe behind a car or under the wooden porch, and waited for Primus to come out again. And later Primus came out.

"The man jumped out and grabbed Daddy's leg and then Robert shot him," Agnes said. The man bled in their front yard but didn't die there. In the end he did die from that gunshot wound, but neither Agnes nor Roy could recall further details of that mill-village shooting. Both brother and sister, however, said that Robert Davis was not charged for any crime in connection with killing that man who had grabbed Primus.

Agnes didn't want to have her daddy shot, but she hasn't forgotten the way he was.

"Daddy didn't do nothin' but loaf," she said.

Roy, Agnes, and their mother Ollie all worked in the mill, not Primus. He did accept a job there once but never finished a whole day's work. Primus worked for a few hours, ran out of the mill and jumped over the fence that encircled it. He was gone and would not return.

"Daddy called the mill a 'slave house,' " Agnes said. "He said, 'that job was made for mules.' "

Hard-working-plowing-the-earth mules, maybe, but thousands of mill workers in Georgia and elsewhere on this land were doing crippling work to feed hungry bellies. There was work and food for mill hands and not much else. And love, if you could make it and keep it.

Back on the Baker County land before the family moved to the Albany mill village in hopes of a kinder world, Ollie, the mostly-exhausted mother, was struggling to guide the mule through rows of prickly cotton plants. Primus did other things but he was not a hard worker.

"She had to do all the field work," Agnes said, as if she was waiting for someone else from those hard-living and hard-dying days to say, "It wasn't really that bad." But no one did.

When she was little, Agnes hoed cotton under a pounding southern sun and pulled peanuts in the fall, when a cool wind would brush her dirty face. Her brothers and sisters worked nearby, little hands and bodies bending and bending and pulling and pulling as if they were being punished for committing some terrible crime. They could look up, shield their eyes from the red-fire ball, and see their mother. Ollie, who had the children and suffered through the miscarriages, plowed the land daylong, and with nightfall she cooked and cared for her working children until her own hands forever ached. When sleep came to Roy's family and wearied bodies lay motionless, dreams carried them to a magical world. It would be a world where a family's labor would be honored. A world they would never find.

Sometimes on Saturdays Primus would take Roy and his brothers hunting, giving them a shotgun and only two shells.

"If we didn't kill, we didn't eat," Roy said. Rabbits, squirrels, possums, raccoons, and most any other animal would eventually be cooked over the fireplace.

Ollie liked to fish and was fond of the small bream or pan fish that she caught in meandering brown waters of the Nochaway Creek. With a cane pole and Roy sitting next to her along the creek bank and helping remove the fish from her hook, Ollie found elusive moments of pleasure and relaxation in that time of forgetting what it's like to suffer behind the mule.

"Momma gutted, scaled, and poked out the eyes," Roy said of the fish before she fried them. They were golden and crisp and white inside, and Roy could eat a hundred of them. Roy Davis loved to go fishing with his mother, both of them away from the red fields and white plants and the agony of it all.

"Back then, there was no time to play," Roy said. "All we done was work. You understand what I'm sayin'?"

No, it's difficult to understand the physical and mental life of a boy working 12 hours a day, pulling, heaving, picking, lifting and doing it all over again and again. Roy would strap a large burlap sack to his waist and walk endless rows of cotton, and when his hands bled, wipe them on the sack and keep picking. This was not my childhood of fun and baseball and a father who loved me and taught needed discipline. Not the Primus kind of discipline.

"How many hours a day did you work, Roy?" I said.

"Worked from sun 'til sun," Roy said. "Daddy whipped us with the bullwhip if we didn't."

Roy evoked a common sharecropper's saying and one used by slaves while describing his work-day schedule when he was a boy. They worked from sun up to sun down, "sun 'til sun." Sometimes the work might continue if a beautiful Georgia full moon lit the fields below. In the book, *Brother, Can You Spare a Dime?* Chronicling life during the Great Depression, there is a photograph of a young African American boy taken near Americus, Georgia, about 60 miles from Roy's home. The boy's clothes are tattered as if someone had been ripping them apart each night, and he's behind a plow being pulled by a mule. The caption reads that the boy is "thirteen and long out of school." He had shifted his body forward leaning with cockiness as he stared directly into the camera. The author used the phrase, "From can see to can't see" in describing the work of southern sharecroppers. The life Roy had been living.

Roy Davis never read a book in his life. But there were many days of unending struggle when he began work at first light and stopped only when he could no longer see.

Roy did other things on the land, whatever Primus told him to do. When Roy was about nine or ten, he and Primus hitched a car ride from Baker County into Albany. In Albany Primus took Roy to a junkyard and bought a tire and a wheel for his Model-T Ford. It was Roy who got them back to Baker County.

"I pushed that sucker all the way back," Roy said. "*Daddy,* I was tired! But I was awright, Daddy. I was awright."

THREE

Near Ichauway Creek, one of the creeks where Ollie Davis caught those small fish that made her happy, was another world, one of diamonds and gold. In 1929 Robert Woodruff, who was making millions of dollars as owner of the Coca-Cola Company bought 29,000 acres of land in Baker County where he and his friends would hunt quail. There were other tracts of land like this in Southwest Georgia, a region streaked with poverty, where the ultra-wealthy came to hunt, drink liquor, and have many servants attend to them. Their neighbors were families like Ollie and Primus Davis.

The Woodruff land by the mid-1990s had become the Joseph W. Jones Ecological Research Center at Ichauway. Named after a senior vice president of the company, scientists today there study the longleaf pine ecosystem, wetlands, and the many animals within the Baker County forest. By 2006 there were more than 100 employees and 25 graduate and undergraduate students from regional universities researching this area to protect the land's natural resources.

There is more concern today for the trees and animals of the land than those who worked and died on it during the time of Roy Davis.

•••••

Sister Agnes remembers Roy, both as a child and a man, at work. "He just worked all the time...*all* the time," she said, in the same manner that you might tell someone what time it is.

Agnes was lying on a recliner at her Albany home during one afternoon wearing a nightgown, and a tube from an oxygen tank had been placed in her nostrils to help with breathing. She was in her 80s.

She began work in the mill when she was seven or eight. She couldn't recall exactly when. "I helped my momma who couldn't hold down her job," Agnes said. Not being able to hold her job down meant that Ollie Davis couldn't physically keep up the crushing pace of work that had been assigned to her. Ollie's job was to feed spools of thread into looms. The thundering looms were fast, monotonous. Life killers they could be.

"Here, Momma, here's another one! I'll help you, Momma!" little Agnes said by her mother's side. She used her tiny, young, and dirty hands to lift spools as the sound of looms exploded and lint engulfed her body. No flowery dresses, dancing lessons, or summer camps. The children worked so the family could eat.

"When you couldn't hold your job down, the bosses fired you," Agnes said.

Ollie Davis earned about three dollars and 65 cents a week working six days a week, Sunday off, from seven in the morning to six in the evening. If her memory is not exact in her time of living between the earth and ether, our land's labor history is both clear and savage. In the 1920s and '30s American mill workers routinely worked for a few cents an hour and sometimes more than 60 hours a week. Hellish work indeed.

Agnes may not have been aware of Ella May Wiggins, who worked in a mill in Gaston County, North Carolina, but their stories have similar verses. In the late 1920s Ella May was earning about nine dollars a week for 70 hours of work. Like Agnes, she had Sundays off. Unlike Agnes, Ella May became involved in efforts to unionize mill workers. Ella May was married to John Wiggins and they had eight children with four dying in early childhood. During pregnancies she continued to work 12-hour shifts in the mill to help feed her family.

On September 14, 1929, while riding in a truck to Gastonia, North Carolina, to attend a union meeting, she was shot and killed by an armed mob. A trial followed for those charged, probably hired by mill bosses, who were acquitted in less than 30 minutes of jury deliberation. She was 29 and her words of *Mill Mother's Lament* spoke about Agnes, Lucy Carnes, and mill mothers throughout the land:

> We leave our home in the morning
> We kiss our children goodbye
> While we slave for the bosses
> Our children scream and cry.
>
> And when we draw our money
> Our grocer's bill to pay
> Not a cent to keep for clothing
> Not a cent to lay away.
>
> And on that very evening
> Our little ones will say
> I need some shoes, dear mother
> And so does sister May.
>
> Now it grieves the heart of a mother
> Everyone must know
> But we cannot buy for our children
> Our wages are too low.
>
> Now listen to the workers
> Both women and you men
> Let's win for them the victory
> I'm sure twill be no sin.

Little Agnes had work to do at home before her teenage years, cooking meals while standing on top an empty fruit crate in order to reach the stove. By 16 she thought she had found happiness and a way out of the life she had been born into. She married Joe Deason Moore in 1936. He was in his early 20s.

"I thought I was gettin' in heaven," she said of her marriage. "I got in hell." Her dream became stale like a mill girl's last piece of bread. "I didn't know nothin' about being married."

Joe Deason Moore, said Agnes while breathing sometimes hard with the oxygen tube in her nostrils, avoided work like it was a fatal disease. They had seven children while Agnes spent the next few decades, at various periods, working in the mill. She once worked 98 hours in one week and earned about 200 dollars. It almost crushed her.

"I never did that again," she said.

She was fired from the mill in the late 1940s after becoming pregnant. Mill bosses knew that her productivity at work because of the pregnancy would eventually be diminished. But babies come and years disappear. Some years later the mill re-hired her, but by the early 1970s she injured her foot on the job and would not return again. She earned no pension. Roy Davis, through 40 years of work, was provided about 100 dollars a month when he retired.

"We didn't even get convict pay," Agnes said.

"Why did you keep working at the mill under those conditions?" I said.

"A lot of times you have to have a high school education to get a good job," Agnes said. "We didn't have one. We didn't know much 'bout readin' and writin'."

A mother must feed her children.

Agnes eventually divorced her husband and none of her children ever worked in the mill.

"I told 'em not to," she said.

•••••

After Roy and Anna Davis married in 1938, they moved into a mill village house with Anna's family. There was Lucy, the always-working mother, her brother C. H., and her sister Rena. There was work, food, and hope. Roy's mill job paid close to five dollars a week for 60 hours of work. It was hard and loud and tiresome but better than the Baker County fields.

"The mill was better 'cause you worked 10 hours a day," Roy said, not the 12 or more that little Roy, fearing his daddy's bullwhip, worked in the fields. Through his decades of millwork Roy worked mostly maintenance. But his first paycheck disappeared like lint in a wind storm.

"He didn't draw one dime the first week we were married," Anna Davis said. Her new husband had bought her so many treats, RC Colas and Snowballs, which were marshmallow and coconut cakes, from the mill store that after the money he owed was deducted from his paycheck, there was nothing left. Anna was not happy. But she knew Roy loved her.

About the time Roy's full love and marriage was beginning, his father and mother's was ending. The wheeler-dealer Primus had left and divorced Ollie to be with a woman who was much younger than the one he had left. Physical ache from life and toil and heart brokenness all over this land had covered Ollie. Primus remarried and the two of them would have four children. When Primus died in 1965, he willed the few acres of land he owned in Baker County to his second group of children. Roy received only a gun after his father's death. He wasn't certain if it was the same one used by his brother, Robert, when he accidentally shot Roy in the head. Primus' second wife, Myrtle, was living in Baker County in 2002 when I drove Roy there to visit the hard land where he was born. Primus and Myrtle had married in 1939, recalled Roy. Myrtle was 25 and Primus 55.

Back in the Albany village by the late 1930s, Roy and Anna rented part of a mill house on their own, away from Anna's family. Anna tried millwork, but she didn't stay long.

"It was *too* much for me," Anna said. There would be work enough at home.

The company allowed mill families land enough to plant a small garden and Anna's hands dug the earth under the sun that made life within the mill miserable. There were peas, peppers, squash, and tomatoes. Food from the mill owners' dirt was grown to feed the hungry Roy and later their children. There were hogs in the village and Anna and Roy would own a few, some for eating and others for selling.

"She sold 'em hogs herself," Roy said. "That was her money. Boy we had a *good* time if ya stop and think about it."

But soon he was called back to the land of his boyhood.

·····

Not many months after Roy and Anna had moved away from her family, Primus became sick on his Baker County land. His father asked Roy to come help on the farm and he did. Roy and Anna returned, with all their dreams of a better life in the Albany mill village, returned to the earth itself and what went in and came out of it. For both of them the move evoked pain. They went anyway.

A few miles from where Roy was born in a sharecropper's shack and closer still to another fragile wooden house he had lived in as a young boy, Roy and Anna set out to homestead. On land that Primus owned, Roy entered the piney woods, selected choice trees, cut them down with a handsaw, and loaded them on a mule-pulled wagon and drove them to a nearby sawmill. Those trees would become home. The mule hauled the fresh pine lumber with the smell of sweet resin back to a piece of land where thick trees and underbrush rose from the earth. They would be near the farming fields and a short walk from Primus' house. He aimed to help the daddy who cracked the bullwhip.

By the early 2000s when I took Roy on one of our trips visiting the land of his boyhood in Baker County, the one-room pine house he had built for Anna and himself was still standing. It was 20 feet by 10 feet with a tin roof and redbrick fireplace. The wood was chipping away through time, animals, and neglect. But there it was standing like a monument reminding us of heroic action. The outhouse or "sugar shack" was gone. During this time of loving and working they drew water from a well that Roy said was once "a little walk up thar," as he pointed to tall brown grass a few yards from where they had built. A man builds himself a life with his hands and his heart.

Back on the farm Roy cut pine for lumber, plowed behind a mule, and picked cotton, as he had done as a little boy. Anna worked, too, as hard as she ever had. She grew vegetables, picked cotton sometimes, carried water, cooked over a fireplace, and hand-washed Roy's red-dust covered clothes in a beaten tub. There was tenderness and toughness over this land.

When Roy returned to help Primus, he was about 30 and if he no longer feared his father, he remembered both the sting of the bull-whip and the nightly taste of moonshine when he was a boy. A man can sometimes be mighty mean to his own son, but if within that meanness there's a forgiving boy and a father who teaches discipline, work, and how to shoot a gun, the boy may come to recognize some of himself in that father. All little boys want to love and deeply know their fathers. Roy was no different. On the farm it was work from "sun 'til sun," a life he thought he had gotten away from.

I walked into the shack that day with Roy. I'm six feet tall and the roof was only a few inches above my head. Roy had gone in before me. It was the first time he had been inside since he and Anna left some 60 years earlier. Roy was quiet for a minute as he stared directly into the fireplace as if it were still burning and he and the young Anna were snuggled around it staying warm and loving one another in a determined way, like a bending pine that had survived its first tornado. Its smallness indicated a place that someone who had done something terribly wrong was forced to remain in. It would be their first home all to themselves.

"Yep, thar's the house me and Momma built," Roy said now looking away from the fireplace along the four walls and en-croaching ceiling. "It was awright for me and Momma. It was awright, I reckon."

I never heard Roy call his wife, Anna. She was always "Momma."

Out of the mill and back on the farm to help Primus, Roy would think about earlier years when he planted, pulled, and picked the life out of the earth. He had been with his mother, Ollie, and his brothers and sisters, all scraped and bleeding from working long in the fields. Now he was back but with Anna this time. She knew the sorrow that life could bring, having come off a farm herself in Crisp County after her daddy ran away from his family. Primus had done the same to his. Anna would never see her daddy again, but Roy had returned to help his.

Along with the tiresome work on the farm with Primus, there were moments when what they stood on, what was around them, and what was above offered repose from the hardness of their world. Here they could experience the redemptive powers of the wooded, misty creeks, and the animals that abound in them. Here the mockingbird sings with melodic beauty. Red-tail hawks fly easily over the planted fields looking for mice and other animals they can kill, carry, and eat. Whitetail deer leap over wire fences from one field to another eating both at the hand of God and the hand of man, and the crops he had planted. Rain falling on Roy and Anna's tin roof in their tiny pine home could've been calming in its rhythm as it turned red fields green with life and hope. An orange spring sun, when wildflowers bloom and bees hover over them, slides gently between tall pines, disappearing with the same grace as an old comforting friend who you will soon see again. Roy and Anna were living in this world of mystery and mist.

FOUR

Roy would leave Primus and the land and join the navy about the time World War II came to America December 7, 1941. He was sent to Illinois for training and then to Norfolk, Virginia, where he would be stationed for about four years. Roy worked as a security guard on base and didn't serve overseas. He would see places and things in America he had never seen before and would never see again.

Part of his monthly paychecks he sent home to Anna, who had their first child, Elmo Mae, in 1940. With Roy gone, Anna and child moved back to the Albany mill village living with Anna's mother, Lucy Carnes. Roy's military memories were not many.

"I was treated awright" by the navy, Roy said. "The ones in the navy that couldn't read got their paychecks first."

He missed Anna mightily and said that, "I wrote her every day." Actually he dictated his letters to one of his navy buddies, and then signed slowly, carefully before mailing them home.

Anna missed Roy equally and she traveled a few times to see him while he was stationed in Virginia. On her first trip she took Elmo Mae. The train plowed north leaving the crimson soil behind. It was the first time his angel had left Georgia.

"I was scared," Anna said. But as the train came out of Georgia and into the Carolinas she began to enjoy the ride and what she saw through the window. She held Elmo Mae tight as the train crossed river bridges and farm fields across the horizon.

In Columbia, Charleston, and Wilmington were homes of wealthy families who had many things bought with money, things

25

Roy and Anna would never have. She would've seen poverty along the way similar to her own. She saw the Atlantic Ocean and its vastness. She had nothing to compare it to.

Before arriving in Norfolk, both Anna and Elmo Mae had fallen asleep on the train. The window next to their seat had been left open allowing smoke from the train itself to enter the car. In her sleep and dreams Anna felt secure, eager to see the man she loved.

"When I seen Roy, we was black," Anna said, all covered with smoke from the train. "I was so embarrassed."

Roy remembered it the same.

"They was a tiny bit dusty," he said. "The coal smoke made 'em black as an ace of spades."

They were dusty, but he was happy to see Anna and their first child. Roy secured a garage-apartment for them for the next few weeks and they talked and loved one another the same way they had done at the mill village. They touched the great saltwater and saw giant ships with powerful guns that had traveled to faraway places.

They did things together that they had always done. Anna brought some comic books for Roy. He couldn't read them, but Anna could. She had gone to school little but had learned to read some when she was young.

Roy's favorite comic books were about western heroes, Lash LaRue and Roy Rogers. He listened intently as Anna, sometimes taking a few moments to correctly pronounce a word, read of Roy Rogers on a swift horse riding the Great Plains, shooting his gun to save the weak and honest from the mean and powerful.

"He'd know when I skipped a word," Anna said. "He'd say 'go back and read 'em over.'"

"Yep, I loved Roy Rogers," Roy Davis said of the same cowboy hero I watched on black-and-white televisions of the 1960s.

On base Roy was the catcher for the baseball team. The farm and millwork had toughened his stout body, a good foundation for a catcher.

"I were a good un, too," he said.

Roy was hit in the head by a swinging batsman, crouching next to the hitter, during one game and was hospitalized for a few weeks. He had lost much of his memory of the life he had lived because of the accident. Navy doctors kept in contact with Anna during Roy's recovery and hospital stay. Her worries did not stop. Her own father walked away from her family and now what would she do if she lost Roy or if he would be physically unable to provide for her? What would she do?

"They had me in the crazy ward," Roy said. "I couldn't 'member nothin'."

Roy fully recovered and by 1946 was honorably discharged from the military. He hitchhiked from Virginia home to Anna, Elmo Mae, and his first son, Leroy, born in 1945.

Roy returned to the mill.

"Them mill bosses gave us two rooms at the village when Roy got out," Anna said.

She loved and held her man, like so many times before.

••••

Before Leroy was born, Anna had given birth to Hubert, but he only lived a few weeks. After Leroy, Roy and Anna had Bobbi and Timmy in the years following the war. In the early 2000s Leroy, Bobbi, and Timmy were all living in Albany or on its outskirts. Elmo Mae, by this period, had died a few years earlier. Bobbi would follow their father into the Flint River Cotton Mill, but she didn't stay long. Leroy lived in the mill village but never worked in the mill. He has worked for more than 30 years at Coats & Clark Inc. in Albany, a plant that processes wool.

Leroy wore dark-rimmed glasses like his daddy, kept his hair cropped military-short, like Roy. He remembered the village, unlike Anna and her mother Lucy Carnes, as a place where he and other boys had fun. He played baseball, sometimes worked in the family garden and sometimes went to school, but not much, and took food to his father at the mill. When his mother needed help in their house, Leroy provided it. This was not Roy Davis' boyhood.

"I reckon you could call it a shotgun shack," Leroy said. "You could look through the front door straight through the backdoor."

A wood stove was in the kitchen for heating and cooking, single bedroom, and a living room. A toilet had been installed on the back porch near a spigot where water was drawn for cooking, drinking, and bathing. A large sink was in the kitchen where "Momma probably bathed me," Leroy said.

He got dirty picking blackberries, working the garden, and playing baseball with the mill children in a vacant field in the village, with tattered gloves and ragged balls. A mill girl once accidentally swung a bat, smashing Leroy in the head. He was not hospitalized like his father before him.

"That bat 'bout *kilt* me," Leroy said. A mill nurse, who cared for workers and their families, treated Leroy.

While Leroy was playing, his daddy was working.

"I used to take Daddy's lunch to the mill," Leroy said. "He always worked a lot of hours, but I never heard him complain."

After playing in the village, Leroy walked through a cow pasture to his grandmother's house. "Ollie lived in a shack. I *mean* a shack," Leroy said. After Primus left her, Ollie "took up" with Robert Barnett, a man the family didn't recall many details about, except one. Barnett was a moonshiner and was killed in an automobile crash in Florida while being chased by the law. There were moonshine runners and fast cars, and dead men on the highways.

After a hog had been slaughtered at Ollie's, barrels of salted-meat were stored in the corners of her home. This was too much for a hungry boy to resist.

"I remember just breakin' off a hunk of meat anytime I wanted," Leroy said. But it's Primus and his bullwhip that Leroy remembered the most.

I spoke to Leroy at his house on Spring Flats Road, a country drive a few miles south of Albany. When I asked him about Primus, his eyes grew scared. He leaned back in his chair and extended his arms over his head as if to protect himself against another whipping.

"He was just a *mean* man…**MEAN** man!" he said, fearful just in the telling of the Primus story.

Primus, with his dreaded bullwhip, once beat Leroy on his bare ass and legs. Leroy couldn't remember why he was punished in such a way, but he said it could've been because he didn't close a car door exactly how Primus wanted him to.

"Primus didn't speak but one time," Leroy said, still feeling the pain from those lashes. "The second time that whip spoke. He got me good once."

Primus' meanness once kept him out of a hospital when he needed medical help. He had gotten hurt or had become sick, Leroy wasn't sure which, and his family took him to a hospital. Primus refused to enter the hospital without his gun, maybe the same .38 caliber pistol that was mistakenly fired into Roy's head. Doctors in turn refused to treat him if he brought the gun inside. Primus left without the treatment.

"He didn't trust anyone," Leroy said.

With Leroy and Elmo Mae playing in the village, Roy and Anna began saving money to buy some land and build a home. Anna sold hogs to help. By the early 1950s they had borrowed about 500 dollars from a bank to buy some land to build a home on. The property was on Sixteenth Avenue, about a mile from the mill. Anna was more determined than Roy to buy the land. She worked hard at saving and made the necessary business arrangements. She wanted out of the village and into their own home. No more mill bosses as landlords.

"Momma wanted her own home," Roy said. "I reckon it was time to leave the village."

Roy could not read nor write, Anna could read some, but they would do it themselves with their children working beside them.

Some folks laughed at them, saying they could never build a home on their own. But they did. Roy, Anna, and the children searched for pieces of discarded lumber at building sites. Watkins Lumber Company in Albany gave them pieces to use. One of Roy's mill hands gave them glass for windows. They spent sparingly. They had little to spend.

After his shift ended at the mill, Roy worked on *their* piece of land with Anna next to him and Elmo Mae sometimes helping, other times caring for younger brother Leroy. Anna became pregnant but worked on the house anyway. She would become nauseated from her pregnancy while working and walk to the nearby trees and underbrush to vomit. She'd then returned to building her house. Maybe her mother's, Lucy Carnes, and her own hopes were being realized. The crying little girl from Crisp County abandoned by her father now lived in a better world.

Roy and Anna worked until dark, and if the moon was bright they continued. They sweated and strained together to have their own house. They owned the land, and the house was made whole by pieces found and pieces given to them. Their lives were improving. Within them each, pride was replacing anxiety. It took them about a year to build what they called, and still call today, "the Pink House" because for years and years it had been painted pink. By the early 2000s, when Roy's granddaughter and great-granddaughter were living in it, the house was still pink. Roy and Anna, when I interviewed them, were living in another house called the Big House that was later built next to the Pink House.

It was simple, the Pink House, one room only and no electricity in the beginning, but it would come later. They bought coal from the mill and burned it in a potbelly stove for cooking and heating. In the backyard was an outhouse or "sugar shack." There was no indoor plumbing and the children walked about 200 yards to a pump to fill their buckets with water and returned home.

Bobbi was born in 1950 around the time the family had completed the house. Five of them now were living in the one-room house, 24 feet by 24 feet, with a tin roof. Bobbi recalled the pasteboards on the ceiling and the potbelly stove. "That was all the heat we had," she said. There was no privacy and no closets, but there were bunk beds for children. Let the people laugh. By God Almighty they built it themselves.

Bobbi saw Roy walk to work at the mill, and she sometimes "walked daddy's lunch to him." Over the years they might own a car, sometimes not.

"If you didn't make enough money to fix them when they tore down they'd sit," Bobbi said.

The family would get electricity but Roy couldn't recall exactly what year it came. "We were the first house to get it over here in our neighborhood," Roy said. Life was getting better still. A few years later Timmy was born. Now there were six of them in the one-room house of scrap lumber, a family built on love, sweat, and the acceptance of unrequited labor.

FIVE

Through the 1950s and '60s America was experiencing the post-World War II economic rise in many parts of the nation, professional historians write. Throughout the war years and following them, a substantial middle class was developing. Manufacturing jobs propelled this shift. There were steel mills in Pittsburgh, auto plants in Detroit, Atlanta and other cities offering fair paying jobs for 40 hours of weekly work. There was usually health care and a secure retirement that many of these companies provided for workers. Union membership, increased demand for manufacturing goods here and abroad, and a steel-nosed work ethic among Americans all contributed to the rising middle class and the secure comforts they were able to realize.

None of this held for southern mill workers.

Roy Davis had been living in a working-poverty life from the fields of Baker County to the Albany mill. He, along with many other whites and blacks from the Deep South, did not experience the post-war prosperity of other manufacturing workers. Many mill workers remained un-unionized as they made a few mill owners very wealthy. Write all you want about the country's post-war boom, it remained a bust in southern mills.

Long after slavery and sharecropping ended in the South, the motivation for both, greed and oppression, remained twin monsters that haunted the land. Roy's working world, like many others in southern mills, was unskilled and uneducated. The sweat-drenched labor of Roy and many others would never be honored.

If it's true that on this earth a man has only two things to offer, his love and his labor, Roy's time speaks like an ancient oracle. The frail Anna accepted that love many years ago, a young mill girl in a hard and unforgiving time. She loved him back in the bearing of children and the caring for him, in the piney woods, in the mill village, and later inside the Pink House. He had dropped his sweat on the land and onto the mill floor, for little pay, sustained by the cling-to-the earth love he had given to Anna, and what he had found in return.

•••••

Leroy, before beginning three decades of factory work in Albany at Coats & Clark Inc., had gone to work as a teenager. Not in the Flint River Cotton Mill where Leroy was doggedly determined to stay out of. Like his daddy, he got little schooling.

"I never got out of grammar school," Leroy said.

By 16 Leroy was working on a Lee County farm and at a gas station owned by Lou Williams. Roy worked at the same gas station a few hours a week, one of several part-time jobs he took over the years to supplement his mill pay.

"Daddy would finish his shift at the mill and come to the station," Leroy said. "And me and Lou would go fishin'. Daddy just worked all the time…*all the time.*"

With Roy often away from the children, it was Anna mostly who disciplined them. She had been tempered by the hardness of her early days and the struggles she had overcome with Roy. She would be stern but loving with her own children, ever mindful of the days when it seemed that the whole damned world had conspired against her. Maybe it had.

The children would behave themselves and respect their parents while learning the discipline of work. Anna would see to it. She worried about Roy drinking too much hard liquor like other men in his family and the ruination they had brought on themselves. Roy befriended a black man who worked on a garbage pick-up route and sometimes brought Roy moonshine, the taste of his youth. There were alcoholics enough in Roy's family.

"My daddy would've been an alcoholic if not for my mother," Bobbi said. "She may've been little but she was tough."

Leroy agreed with his sister.

"Momma would tear your ass up in a heartbeat," Leroy said. "Daddy would whip us but not like Momma." Leroy had felt the sting of Primus' whip and little Anna, tough, tough Anna, was not abusive but swung a mighty leather strap.

Roy never spanked Bobbi but did fake it a few times. Sometimes Anna would tell Roy to whip Bobbi for misbehaving.

"He'd take me to the bedroom and hit the bed and tell me to scream," Bobbi said. "Then he'd give me a dollar. Momma's the one who'd tear the blood out of you. You didn't cross Momma."

Roy had endured the wrath of Primus' whip, but from his own hands to his own children, this was not to be. Anna's whippings were hard, a reminder of the world they were living in. Maybe her whippings were hopeful and instructive acts that her children would make a better world for themselves. Roy Davis had grown up in the unforgiving world where landowners and mill owners paid shameful wages for life-exhausting work. Roy lived with tenderness that Primus rarely if ever revealed. The fact that Roy found it difficult and at times simply impossible to whip his own children was both a sickening reminder and rejection of the ways of Primus. Roy embodied something else, something soft and kind. It may have come from his mother Ollie and his grandmother, Lizza Davis, who kept little Roy warm by the fireplace during cold winter nights in a wind-blown shack.

Angels can do that, too.

•••••

When Bobbi was about 15, during the mid-1960s, she fell in love and married a 22-year-old marine from California who was stationed at the Albany base. Bobbi never went to high school but moved to California with her new husband. A divorce soon followed. She met another man there, became pregnant, had the baby but didn't marry the child's father.

On the west coast Bobbi found "a good-paying job" in Newport Beach working for an aircraft company. The plant overlooked the Pacific Ocean.

"I loved going to work and getting off and looking out over the ocean and seeing the sailboats," Bobbi said. "I wondered what those people did for a living."

The job was good, the weather and water beautiful, but she longed for her momma and daddy. By 1973, about the time I was working under Roy at the mill, Bobbi and her baby girl came home to Albany to live with her parents.

During the mid-1970s Roy and his family bought a pre-manufactured house and added other rooms to it. The Pink House of the early 1950s was next to it. Elmo Mae and her husband would live in the new house or Big House with Roy and Anna. Soon though Elmo Mae's marriage went terrible and before that divorce, Anna saw her oldest daughter faint more than once because of physical abuse from her husband. Now Bobbi and her baby moved into the Big House. There were times when Anna had ten beds in the new house, always there to help her children and grandchildren when they had fallen.

Roy asked the mill bosses to hire Bobbi and they did. Bobbi worked at that "wild place" for about three years. But she could endure no more.

"I was lucky my dad got me a job at the mill," Bobbie said laughing about it all now years later. "I thought slavery days were over."

She longed for the better working conditions and good pay that she had left in California. The soft Pacific breeze she found only in her memories. The mill paid her minimum wage for work as "filler." She filled the giant looms with spools of thread. The work was hard and repetitive. And you could be killed.

During one shift she saw a spool, or what was also called a needle, fly off a machine striking a co-worker in the neck. It was a serious injury in which the millworker's speech was forever damaged.

"The work was horrible. The bosses were rough," Bobbi said. "They worked you hard."

Mill work was breaking Bobbi as it had done her mother, Anna, some 40 years earlier. It had broken her grandmother, Lucy Carnes, too. Primus, her grandfather, didn't complete one day of work before he left, never going back. Bobbi's aunt Agnes survived several years of the drudgery before getting out. Roy would last nearly four decades. There had been many broken dreams and broken lives.

Bobbi, unlike those in the 1800s who used the Underground Railroad, was planning her escape from "slave work."

Liberation came one day when she purposely didn't fill up the looms with enough spools of thread, knowing that the machine would malfunction and cause a delay in production. It was about noon that day when her machine stopped. Bobbi then went running out of the mill.

"I just ran the hell out of there," she said grinning with the telling of it. "I had planned this to a *T*. I wanted my boss to suffer."

She never went back into the mill.

With no job, Bobbi received financial help from Roy and Anna so she could attend a local technical college. She later became a beautician, her job when I interviewed her in the early 2000s. She would marry Ritchie Buffi, and by the mid-1970s they had two girls and had adopted another. One of their daughters, Sheresse, was born December 22, Roy and Anna's wedding anniversary.

SIX

A century before Roy Davis was born in Baker County, whites there and throughout Southwest Georgia had begun organizing militias to drive out the Muscogee or Creek Indians. It had been their land for centuries. But the seductive lure of cotton had begun permeating this land. By 1836 Albany was founded, and two years later the first "cotton box" would float down the Flint River. The box probably carried 360 bales, each weighing a few hundred pounds, from Albany to Apalachicola, Florida. It cost cotton farmers two-and-a-half dollars to transport each bale. By the 1850s both Albany and cotton production were growing. In 1853 the Georgia General Assembly passed a bill making Albany, originally part of Baker County, part of a new county, Dougherty.

Before the bill was passed, an Albany newspaper reported that when the Baker County Superior Court was in session "almost the entire population of our place is at Newton, detained from business at the great expense of time, money and patience. Such a state of things is intolerable. Our county is entirely too large. Justice demands a change and we hope we shall have it."

New settlers were pushing into Albany and Dougherty with dreams of "white gold" and the prestige and power that such wealth brings. They were coming from Virginia, the Carolinas and from other places where their dreams and the land itself, over used and over farmed, had played out. These newcomers ascribed to the southern code, amassing land and slaves meant wealth and political influence.

By the summer of 1839, William Q. Atkins, much impressed of what he saw here, wrote to his father in Virginia about land that would become Dougherty County:

> This country is settling very fast with wealthy and respectable people...I think in a few years this country will be hard to beat for society or wealth. The land is mostly pine with little or no undergrowth and covered with beautiful grass which enables the people to raise any quantity of cattle. There is no difficulty in clearing land. You only have to fell the trees or simply chop around them, cut timber enough around the edges to fence it in and then go plowing.

Roy Davis and others who worked back-achingly hard would never become part of the "wealthy and respectable people." Roy's sharecropping and millwork were never honored properly by respectable people. It would be the history of this land.

Atkins encouraged his father to come to Southwest Georgia writing that, "You could make more here farming in one year than you could there in five."

James Oakes, in *The Ruling Race: A History of American Slaveholders,* quotes Atkins and others like him who were being lured to the cotton belt, with promises of wealth and prestige. Oakes writes of the urgent tone in the letters written by those desiring what the land holds. Come here, a place where your dreams could be realized.

Oakes writes, I quote the spelling exactly, this in regards to the urgency:

> The climax of these enticements was the evitable and invidious comparison between West and East. Distinctions were commonly drawn in multiple, the new country being so many times better than the old. Of Tennessee's superiority over North Carolina: "I can do better hear then I can thear & work half my time Sally can make more hear in three months then she can thear in twlve." Of Mississippi over South Car-

olina: "You can repair your affairs in one year here as much as you can there in three." Of Louisiana over Georgia: "One Negro hear will make you more than four will in Georgia."

For as long as there was slavery, masters wrote with this kind of eagerness and exaggeration, longing for wealth through land and cotton, Oakes writes. White Gold would become the only export grown from these cleared fields, picked with enslaved hands. East of the Flint River, tobacco was grown and there was even some limited sugar cane production in the fertile lands around Albany. But for those whose letters and diaries Oakes has read, they came for the cotton and brought slaves do to the work.

The 1854 Dougherty County tax digest recorded about 4,000 slaves valued at more than two million dollars, almost 40 percent of the county's taxable wealth. A few "Negroes" were listed as freed before the Civil War began in 1861.

Fewer than half of adult white males in Dougherty owned slaves. Most who did owned fewer than ten, as was common throughout the South. There were a few southern white men who owned enough to operate a large nineteenth-century factory. Five hundred and sixty slaves were owned by Joseph Bond, a landowner in Dougherty and neighboring counties. Slavery, as early as the 1840s, had become entrenched in the Albany economy with local businessman Gabriel Sibley operating a slave auction where the wealthy and respectable could "SELL AND BUY NEGROES and other property on Commission at fair and reasonable rates."

With human bondage comes a terrorizing code of punishment that transcended the life of Roy Davis, born white and free some 50 years after slavery was outlawed in America.

Georgia historian and writer David Williams documents this horrible treatment in his book *Rich Man's War: Class, Caste, and Confederate Defeat in the Lower Chattahoochee Valley:*

> Besides being terribly painful, whipping was for the slaves a key symbol of their lowly status. It is hardly surprising then

that resistance to whipping became one of the main ways slaves sought to demonstrate a measure of independence. Such resistance could, of course, be very dangerous. One Troup County planter was noted for turning his dogs on slaves who refused to be whipped. A slave on the Hines Holt plantation near Columbus was shot after he beat off six men who tried to hold him down.

Whippings may have been the last resort, but they were also the centerpiece of plantation slavery with longstanding cultural influences. More from Williams about the whip and what it meant:

"If the law was to forbid whipping altogether," a Louisiana slaveholder said, "the authority of the master would be at an end." According to one Virginia master "a slave does not do half the work he easily might; and which, by being harsh enough with him, he can be made to do." The truth is, one forthright slaveholder asserted, only compulsion causes men to work. "This compulsion is more readily and fully applied to the black than the white laborer," he argued, "and consequently more work is obtained from the former than the latter."

That pain would be felt for many years and not just by slaves.

•••••

Roy Davis, when he was an old man, still felt the whole hurt of his father's bullwhip. Primus Davis whipped his children and his grandchildren. Roy didn't know if Primus, born in 1884, had been whipped by his father or grandfather, but no one in Roy's family who knew Primus firsthand would dismiss its probability. Coming of age when he did, Primus would've walked in the same light and darkness of former slaveholders who had whipped slaves in the fields. These men used the most common and feared tool on the plantation, and when slavery ended, the whippings did not.

The men of Primus' boyhood lived under a code of regimented terror. It was an alloy to the southern way of life. This violent culture of bondage would come to influence the free and the white. Using the bullwhip on his own children and grandchildren reflected the culture that Primus experienced, one in which racial violence came to influence how some whites would treat one another even within their own families. Roy Davis, though, would never pick up the whip.

With the end of slavery in 1865 and the beginning of sharecropping in Roy's Baker County world, southern life was progressing but abuses remained. The sharecropping system Roy grew up in replaced the slave plantation as the southern model. Planters still owned the land but divided it up into small plots, making it available for freedmen and poor whites alike. This new type of agriculture was also known as crop lien. Through contracts with merchants, typically the landowners themselves, credit and supplies – fertilizer, seed, mules, tools, clothing, shoes, and sometimes food - were provided to the poor in exchange for liens or claims on their harvests. One of the cruelties of the system, besides the hard work and little cash, was that sharecropping families were soon trapped in indebtedness, making it difficult to leave the land based on the contracts they had signed. Poverty and abuse were as common as mules and cotton.

Most sharecroppers, like Roy's family, were illiterate and found themselves prey to owners and the mysteries of money, debt, and interest on that debt. From inside and out it was a rotten system for those who did the crushing work that made landowners wealthy.

In 1910, six years before Roy was born, sharecroppers operated about 40 per cent of the state's 291,000 farms. Sharecropping rates were highest in the counties where cotton was dominant, where much labor was needed. But change would come.

By the late 1920s thousands of sharecroppers throughout the South, like the Roy Davis family, were leaving the cotton picking for the cotton mills. They left to escape the greedy landowners and because cotton harvests were becoming less profitable for owners and pickers alike. The price per pound dropped after World War I ended in 1918 when worldwide demand fell fast. Pickers were hurt again by the boll weevil, the tiny destructive bug that invaded southern fields in the 1920s. There would still be cotton enough and thread and cloth to be made.

•••••

Cotton mill production in the early 20th century began in the opening room where workers removed the ties and bagging from raw bales of cotton. This was done in adjacent warehouses that were dusty and dirty and fire hazards. Machines and workers tore apart the compressed cotton, removing dirt and short fibers. A vacuum system then carried the fluffed cotton through a giant tube to the picker room where pickers, or lappers as they were also known, continued to clean the cotton and organize it in continuous, even sheets.

The next step was for card hands to feed these sheets into carding machines where sharp metal teeth again tore apart the cotton, converting the mass into a continuous sliver, or loosely compacted rope that coiled into cans. Workers then placed the compacted rope through a series of rollers in the head of a drawing frame where they were combined in a single strand. Rollers ran at increasing speed, making the sliver of cotton thinner. The yarn was subject to roving and was slightly twisted. As a result, bobbins on the spinning frames filled with thread while workers referred to as doffers replaced them with empty ones. Other workers known as spinners would quickly move up and down the row of machines, repairing snags.

As the process continued, spoolers ran machines that combined the thread from 10 to 15 different bobbins. Problems arose when the thread broke. Workers could repair broken threads by tying them in a knot. This step created the yarn that could be wound into balls for sale or later used by weavers who processed the yarn further into simple cloth like sheeting. Some mills produced fabric with a variety of patterns and designs.

And in all mills the work for young and old alike was crushing.

•••••

Ragged farmers like Roy, his mother Ollie, and the rest of the Baker County family came to believe that the Flint River Cotton Mill in Albany, despite its kind of misery, was a place of hope. Hope wears a different mask a century removed.

In 1914 *The Atlanta Georgian* editorialized on behalf of children like the ones Ollie was giving life to. The newspaper was advocating reforms in child labor:

> …Our answer was that children are more important than mills, and that the law of any decent state in the Union should prevent this grinding up and burning out of childhood. Child labor conditions in Georgia have long been a disgrace to the state…The South today is richer than the whole United States was at the beginning of the Civil War. We doubt whether a majority of Georgia's slave-owners would have allowed the children of their slaves to be put to work in cotton mills at the age of ten. Black flesh, when owned as a personal asset, was too valuable to be wasted in this fashion.

The editorial praised the Georgia House for voting 99 to 42 prohibiting children under 14 from working in mills and other factories. Working children who could not read or write would attend school 12 weeks a year until they were 16 and then could become a fulltime millworker.

The story continued: The passage was fought by mill owners and their representatives. Its passage is a tribute to the increasing sense of decency and civilization that only 42 men in this body were willing to be counted in opposition to such a measure.

Georgia worked children in mills longer and harder than most states and what few restrictions lawmakers passed in the early 20th century were weakly enforced. Greed and the willingness to steal the labor and sweat from others while offering so little in return had deep roots among those who owned land and capital. Uprooting this would be the work of outsiders. Federal laws of the 1930s and '40s, while President Franklin Roosevelt was in office, would effectively over time end child labor in Georgia and throughout the land. Until then the "grinding up and burning out of childhood" would continue in the Flint River Cotton Mill and others of the South.

For the Atlanta newspaper to support such a bill against the wishes of the wealthy mill owners would have certainly been attacked as the workings of an intrusive government. Cries of "socialism" could be heard from mill owners outraged that the government would now determine who they couldn't hire. What would come next? Laws concerning pay and the number of hours you could work a mill hand? Those whose wealth and power seemed threatened would fight change regardless of how many children they were grinding up.

I was fortunate to have been a child in the 1960s when my father's factory work in Indiana and later Georgia was honored many times more than the work Roy Davis and his family did in the mill. My childhood was one of baseball, fishing, and fun. I never feared a mill boss or worked to physical exhaustion. A 12-year-old boy picking cotton or working ten hours next to the crashing sound of cotton mill looms, covered in heat, lint, and sweat, is foreign to what America should be. It was what America once had been.

From the late 1800s until 1940, cotton textiles was Georgia's leading industry as many mills moved from the northeast to the South. Mills moved to be closer to cotton, saving money that would've been used for shipping the raw materials north. There was cheaper electricity in the South and a milder climate. There's no need to heat already hot mills in the winter and no air conditioning for much of the 20th century. But it was the cheap southern labor that became the strongest attraction for northern mill owners.

Roy Davis and his family and their mill co-workers were willing to work for less money, more hours per day, and sometimes complain little, unlike their northern counterparts. By the 1920s and '30s there was a growing labor movement but primarily in the North. That, in time and with growing mistreatment, would change, too. Until then life in southern mill villages, with all its lint, work, and hope, quietly endured.

These mill villages appeared in cities and larger towns like Albany, and most workers were like the Roy Davis family. They had come off the farm and into the mill villages. The southern villages included company-owned houses, churches, stores, and schools. From *A History of Georgia* published in 1977:

> In 1890 a visitor described rural mill villages as consisting of "rows of loosely built, weather-stained frame houses, all the same ugly pattern and buttressed by clumsy chimneys…" Inside the bare floors were marked with "the tread of animals" and the "muddy outline of splayed toes of all shapes and sizes" of bare-foot people.

Millworkers, the same book reported, labored 70 hours a week for so little pay that children like Roy's sister, Agnes, working alongside their mothers, became mill hands, too. Village life and sharecropping did have similarities. Like the landowner who advanced supplies to a family working on shares, company-owned stores allowed mill families food, medicine, and clothing to be paid for by future wages. Mill workers were sometimes paid not in cash but in "scrip" to be redeemed at the company store.

By the 1940s, and with the coming of World War II, mill life was changing. Wages remained low but new federal laws established both a minimum wage and a standard 40-hour work week. Many mothers and teenagers continued working in mills. About 60 percent of millworkers, like Anna and Roy when he returned from the military, were living in mill villages. Mill houses were beginning to display a variety of colors, and by this period many had electricity and indoor plumbing. These were comforts that Roy and Anna would soon enjoy.

SEVEN

The Albany Cotton Mill was built in 1909 when local investors spent a quarter of a million dollars for construction and looms and other machines needed to process cotton. A few years later the company was sold to Francis Putney, a New Englander who had come to Albany following the Civil War. It was later re-named the Flint River Cotton Mill and operated by the Wetherbee family, which Putney had married into. Three Wetherbee brothers would operate it for years, including in the time of Roy Davis.

On September 4, 1934, with thousands of textile workers on strike nationwide, the *Albany Herald* published this headline - No Pickets at Local Mill Yet: Patrol Continues. Local readers found this in their paper:

> Although a picket "threat," which reached the ears of company officials Monday, had failed to materialize, the ten-man patrol at the Flint River Cotton Mill continued Tuesday, ready to strike at the first indication of disorder. Also ready to lend a hand, should it be needed, were city and county police, who promised to "act first and ask questions afterwards."

> The patrol was organized Monday after mill officials had been told that pickets from a Manchester (Georgia) mill had threatened to invade the local plant. In a speech to millworkers yesterday, Harold Wetherbee, general manager, told the employees that the mill would protect their interests fully and that pickets would not be allowed to molest them or do them bodily harm. The Flint River Mill is among the few in Georgia

where labor troubles have not developed. Mr. Wetherbee said he thought the chances of trouble here were remote but had decided upon the patrol as cautionary measure.

The following day Albany readers learned from an Associated Press story that 200,000 textile workers had walked off their jobs because of low pay and abusive working conditions, including 25,000 in Georgia. Textiles were Georgia's largest industry, then employing more than 60,000 workers. Before the strike ended, 500,000 workers would participate nationwide. Georgia millworkers, briefly, thought that maybe, finally, a political leader was going to help them. They were wrong.

Democratic Governor Eugene Talmadge's primary re-election was scheduled for September 12, as the strike was underway. He gave emotional speeches to cotton mill workers saying, "I will never use the troops to break up a strike." He lied.

After he won the election, Talmadge ordered Georgia's entire National Guard of 4,000 to "arrest the picketers and get the mills back in operation." Soon union leaders were arrested and were not allowed to communicate with fellow workers. Having tricked the workers, Talmadge made the owners happy.

Theodore Forbes, executive secretary of the Cotton Manufacturing Association of Georgia said, "Talmadge is the best governor this state ever had. He broke the strike for us." The strike would end before September did.

Striking workers in Georgia had the help of the United Textile Workers of America and the support of President Roosevelt but they achieved little and endured much violence and death. Five Georgia millworkers were killed, including one beaten to death as his family watched but could not stop the militiamen, on Callaway Mill property near Columbus. Based on newspaper accounts and interviews I conducted, Albany mill workers did not strike and there weren't incidences of violence in connection with it. Fear of reprisals is one reason Albany workers didn't strike, but those in

Augusta, Macon, Griffin, and in other Georgia mills did. It could've been that Albany millworkers lacked organizational leadership necessary for unity among workers while confronted with almost certain violence. Those working days were laced with danger.

What doesn't require speculation during this violent period of the American labor movement is that the act of wanting to improve life by joining a union could and did get people shot.

Throughout that bloody September the *Albany Herald* published headlines like these:

- Two Men Killed in Disorder at Trion Mill in Northwest Georgia
- Augusta Striker Dies of Wounds
- More Than Fifty Mills in State Closed as Strike Enters Third Day
- Six Picketing Strikers Killed in Honea Path

From Honea Path, South Carolina, the story was war-like:

Six picketing strikers were slain and upwards of thirty wounded as guns blazed in a textile strike clash today. The shooting climaxed more than an hour's tension at Honea Path's only textile mill, the Chiquola, after strikers from near-by Belton had come to picket the mill. As the flying squadron (from Belton) arrived here, the plant delayed opening and workers and strikers congregated on the mill grounds. Suddenly, just before 8 a.m., guns began to roar. One striker after another dropped to the ground, dead or wounded. For several minutes, the turmoil continued. No one knows who fired the first shot. Then the strikers retreated – leaving their dead.

Reading this reported carnage in the *Albany Herald* reminded me of cowboy movies that I used to watch as a kid, similar to Roy Davis' infatuation with Hollywood hero Roy Rogers, but at Honea Path real people were dead and wounded. They were bleeding and dying in the hopes of making their lives, and those of unborn workers, better. Throughout the Northeast and the South, profitable mills fought violently to resist unionization. Ten people were dead, 41 injured, and 63 had been arrested after the third day of labor violence. Before it ended, more blood would run.

The strike was called the "most gigantic-walk-out of modern times," but in the end, just a few weeks after it began, little had changed to honor their labor. Representatives from the American Federation of Labor and the United Textile Workers, according to newspaper accounts, said that they won "a method of determining wages upon a basis of fact," and the "practical recognition of our union." The strike produced no immediate relief for most of the nation's millworkers. They would have to wait and endure. For Roy Davis and many like him in southern mills, his hard labor would never be honored.

Mill workers in Albany would never unionize.

•••••

While the local paper reported the nationwide strike, there were other stories on the front page including one about Albany's Chamber of Commerce:

> Few cities, especially cities of the size of Albany are blessed with a Chamber of Commerce so efficient, or which can point to so fine a record of achievements, as the Albany Chamber of Commerce, the attractive offices of which in Hotel Gordon are a veritable bee-hive of activity.

The story reported that a group of "public-spirited citizens" were granted a charter for the chamber in 1911. Officers in 1934 included: Leonard Farkas, president; J. E. LeGreve, vice-president; and Miss Hattie Hardy, secretary. Listed, too, were some wealthy members of the board of directors.

Roy couldn't read the names of Albany's rich chamber members, but in the two years after the story appeared, he began working at the mill. Roy probably never would've been invited to have barbecue and ice cream with these "public-spirited citizens." Nor would he have shared a drink of illegal whiskey with them.

Next to the front page chamber of commerce story was a distinguished illustration of President Franklin Delano Roosevelt, elected in 1932 and then winning the next three presidential elections. Above the picture the editors wrote, "Captain of Our Recovery Program," indicating FDR's New Deal economic programs to help the nation recover from the ongoing Depression. FDR's face as it was depicted in the newspaper was comforting and strong. It evoked authentic humanity. His nose, lips, and chin were perfect in the artist's illustration. Even as a reproduction of a sketch, his eyes were clear and true, a lighthouse helping lost seamen find their way home. Below that face there was suffering.

FDR carried the painful burden of polio and not being able to walk. He suffered physically as the nation and the world did the same. There would be more suffering when the war came to America by 1941. After he took the oath of office in March of 1933, he quickly submitted to Congress numerous pieces of legislation to help a hungry and hurting country. Nearly 25 percent of those who wanted to work could not find work. Hopelessness and despair filled the minds and lives of many. Thousands of people in famous places like New York City waited patiently in line for soup and bread. What they wanted was work and the dignity it brought. For the first time many people in America were experiencing a similar poverty to what Roy at that point had known for most of his life.

Roy Davis could recognize FDR's picture, but he was unable to read about the forthcoming New Deal programs designed to help him and others. By the end of the 1930s, FDR and Congress had passed laws providing a 40-hour work week, the first national minimum wage, Social Security, and rights for workers to unionize and bargain collectively with their employers. Roy and others whose sweat enriched a few were finally, after decades of neglect, being considered by our nation's most powerful.

A few weeks before the president's picture appeared in the paper, a Tifton, Georgia, congressman was quoted in support of FDR's programs, especially Social Security and unemployment insurance. E. E. Cox said this during a speech at the Tift County Courthouse:

> The experience of the Depression has taught us the necessity of finding a more adequate, certain and self-respecting way of taking care of the old and worn out people and of the unemployed who are able to work and want to. It is not sufficient to leave these dependent upon either public or private charity...A bill dealing with these questions is now being constructed and it is expected to be adopted early after the convening of the next Congress.

Cox's phrase "the old and worn out people" was similar to that of the 1914 Atlanta editorial calling for reform in child labor in which there was a "grinding up and burning out of childhood." Workers had been worn out, young and old, because of greed and abusive working conditions. As a result of this and the calamity of the 1930s, some Americans and the government they had created were questioning if capitalism and human decency could co-exist. In Albany there was also talk of another kind of social ill.

Along with stories about the Great Depression, there were concerns expressed of growing public drunkenness. One front page story complained of such local behavior and of liquor being sold downtown in violation of the city's ordinance. Mrs. W. D. Proctor attended a city commission meeting upset about her fellow Albanians.

"The police can catch these bootleggers," she said. "I know they can if they want to." Her tone, as reported in the press, was alarming and anxious. "Something must be done."

Mrs. Proctor gave the commission a list of alleged "dry law" violators in the business district. Mayor R. F. Armstrong reviewed the list and said that most had been tried in court on charges of selling liquor. The "liquor establishment," Armstrong said, had been raided several times but no liquor had been found.

Armstrong offered Mrs. Proctor some perspective on the liquor problem. He had visited Chicago recently, where downtown liquor drinking was legal, and said that he didn't see a "single drunk person." He questioned his own city's logic of prohibiting hard drink.

"The prohibition law cannot be enforced in its entirety," the mayor said. "The federal government spent millions of dollars attempting to enforce it, but never succeeded in eliminating liquor entirely."

Mrs. Proctor had at least one commissioner on her side at the meeting. J. W. Parker said, "I've lived in Albany 13 years, and during the last year, I've seen more drunken men on the streets than ever before."

When Roy Davis was a little boy, his father used to give him a spoonful of moonshine each night before bedtime. Robert was Roy's moonshine brother who was said to have had a still not far from the cotton mill. Roy's mother, Ollie, had a moonshine boyfriend who was killed in a car wreck while the law gave chase. I've seen Roy and other millworkers drink Mellow Corn, which was hard, high-alcohol content legal liquor in the 1970s, straight from the neck in gulps as if it were lemonade on a very hot day. This kind of thing would incapacitate most people. Maybe the drunkenness that J. W. Parker saw partly reflected a whole generation of men slapped down from hard lives and poverty wages, who had found not a friend in the bottle but another bad boss. Maybe not, though.

•••••

For about 20 years beginning in 1980, Phillip McArdle had been president of the Flint River Textile Mill, reflecting yet another name change for the mill. He had been part owner along with some of the Wetherbee family. McArdle was from Dundalk, Ireland, having come to America in 1964 and settled first in New

York. Millwork had been most of his working life. I spoke with McArdle in his office not too long before the mill closed in 2004. It was a hot day in May, one that would've been suffocating inside the mill before it was air conditioned the same year McArdle had left Ireland for America.

He was finely dressed in a tie and plaid sports jacket, and his slacks were pressed straight and smooth. He smoked cigarettes and spoke, with Ireland all around his words, in a careful and articulate way about mills and working in them. The mill was employing under McArdle about 300 workers. The business had changed over the years since Roy Davis worked among the looms. In the 1940s and '50s the mill made material used for bags that held flour. This might have been the same kind of material used by Anna Carnes' mother, Lucy, to make clothes for her children. Pretty clothes, Anna recalled.

Roy had retired before McArdle was hired to run the company, but he knew well of the working conditions Roy and others from his era labored under in mills here and overseas. The heat and the noise of the mills, in the old days, have been eased by air conditioning and quiet modern looms.

"Before it was air conditioned I'm told that the heat in there was really, *really* something," McArdle said. And the looms in those days "generated enormous noise."

McArdle carried himself with a seemingly reserved demeanor, worldly with several books on his shelf. Although Roy had not worked for him, McArdle had heard several stories about the sharecropper from Baker County.

"Apparently he was quite a character," McArdle said.

"Do you know anyone who used to work with him?" I said.

"I think Homer Casey did."

••••

Homer Casey had worked with Roy for many years, and like Roy, Homer had come off the farmland and into the mill village. Homer was born in 1923 in Worth County, about 20 miles east of Albany, but unlike Roy, Homer had been too young to work the land before his family came to the mill. Homer's memories of his father, Jeff Casey, are that of a strong man plowing behind a mule, tilling the land and harvesting its crops.

"I'd follow my father out to the fields and that was about it," Homer said.

I met Homer in the early 2000s where he was working as a security guard at the mill, still 40 hours a week after more than 50 years among looms and lint. He had begun working there in 1943, following his father into the mill. Elder Casey was employed for 25 years in the mill. Millwork had been as rhythmic as the autumn winds: Father and son and mother and daughter and husband and wife.

During Homer's first year in the mill, by then Roy was serving in the navy, he met a pretty mill hand from Florida, Juanita Webb. Juanita was living with her grandmother on Tenth Avenue, a neighborhood today lined with simple A-frame single-family homes and protective, giant, live oak trees planted methodically on both sides of the road, beautiful with Spanish moss and large shading branches. Homer and Juanita courted and married in 1944.

He struggled pronouncing her name, but he had loved her from the beginning.

"I used to spell it with a "W" when I was goin' with her," he said. "She set me straight on that."

He finally got the spelling right, and they've been married ever since. Juanita worked in the mill 40 years before retiring. They had one child, Ronald Homer Casey, who worked in the mill only for a short time, thought about it some, and never went back. When Homer and Juanita married, he was out of the mill and into the army during World War II.

"I didn't go overseas. I had a busted eardrum," he said. "They turned me down on that."

The ever-pounding, ever-thundering of the mighty looms could wear a man thin, both inside and out.

Back in the mill by 1947, Homer said that the conditions "were rough" and he worked a lot of overtime. "Money was short but at the time we made a fair living." He "carried home about 20 dollars" for a week of mill work, including some overtime, but he couldn't recall exactly how many hours he worked. He did recall that, like Roy, he took part-time jobs over the years to supplement his mill pay.

Homer remembered meeting Roy during this period, both young strong men who served their country and returned home to again serve mill owners. They were both married to mill women and would be for a long time.

Homer said "yes sir" to me several times, using the phrase in every other sentence. He said it as often as Roy called me and others "Daddy." I met Homer at noon on a summer day inside the mill's security office. He reminded me of Roy. Homer was short, like Roy, maybe five feet seven. Both men were trim, solid, and muscles from their youth not yet entirely gone. For a man soon to be 80, Homer was impressive. He wore a light blue uniform shirt, and his dark pants were pressed by someone who had taken concern to get everything right. His shirt was short sleeved and of his forearms I saw years of physical work. On his shirt was a badge, and over the badge, on the left side of his chest, was an American flag pin. He wore glasses and his hair, still rather thick, was neatly combed. Homer had brought his lunch to work in a tin pail. It looked like it could've been the same one he used when FDR was president. I saw a sandwich in a plastic bag on his office counter.

"Homer, go ahead and eat," I said.

"Yes, sir, I think I will."

"What do you remember about Roy Davis? Can you tell me some things about him?"

"I knew Roy, you know what I mean? I just worked around him for quite a few years."

They worked in different departments in the mill most of those years but did see each other and speak to one another almost daily, the way Homer recalled it.

"Roy was a good worker, yes sir!"

Homer took a bite of his sandwich and then a drink from a can of Pepsi. He was neat while eating. Nothing would soil *his* uniform. We talked about the mill and he told me what it was like working there after the war and into the 1950s and '60s.

"It's a hundred percent better today," Homer said, "we got air conditionin'."

He took another bite and looked out the security office window, chewed slowly his sandwich. But his words were rapid.

"The whole time I've been here the owners have never mistreated me. No, sir, I can't bring that against 'em."

His voice was sharp and certain with quick sounds, as if he were being surprised by something.

"They've never missed a pay day," Homer said of the mill owners. "They pay me just what they promise and they as good as people I ever met." He said company president Philip McArdle was a "wonderful man."

Homer Casey continued to eat as workers came into the security office and left moments later, asking about things that Homer had the answers to. The office was clean and everything seemed to be where it should have been. Before walking into his office, I had looked through a window and into the mill. I saw many machines, orderly and repetitive. For six decades Homer had been at the mill where thread and yarn have been made from cotton, picked white and soft but pressed into bales, heavy but still white and soft.

By the early 1990s Homer had finally come out of the mill and into the security office where he was earning six dollars an hour. Fifty years later and still he earned *six* dollars an hour. When I met and interviewed Homer, he was up to seven.

Homer Casey was dignified in his uniform and badge telling me about his job and how much he earned and how much he had appreciated mill bosses. He was, it seemed to me, a proud man, proud of what he had accomplished in this world. He and Roy shared lives of work, added together nearly 100 years in the mill, and marriages that totaled 120 years: Love and work and work and love.

Before I said goodbye to Homer Casey, I looked a final time above his heart where he wore the American flag.

EIGHT

When my father woke me up to go to work at the mill at 6:15 Sunday morning, I had only been asleep four hours, and I felt terrible. Leonard Lawless picked me up in his LTD Ford, a big blue machine with fenders as strong as Georgia oak trees. Lawless hadn't gotten much sleep either. He had been with me. We knew Roy Davis would be pissed if we were late, but he could never stay that way for long.

"Let's go *Daddy*," Lawless said as I got into his car carrying a paper bag full of food for lunch. "Roy's waitin' for us and you don't want to be late for your daddy."

"The hell with Roy. I'm tired *Daddy*," I said.

"Now John Boy, don't talk about your real daddy that way," Lawless said.

"John Boy" or "Uncle John" and sometimes "Tall One" were my mill names that Roy had given me when he wasn't calling me and the rest of the lint heads "Daddy." I was a little taller than my mill crew, and about being referred to as John, that was just what Roy Davis called me. All of us lint heads had mill names and we used them even when we were away from the mill. Roy never called us by our real names. I don't think he could remember them. He never forgot our mill names.

"Where's Junior?" I said. "I'm tellin' you I'm tired of him being late. That lint head ain't never ready on time."

"No, he ain't ready," Lawless said. "We gotta go back and get 'em."

Joey "Junior" LaMoy lived next door to Lawless on Whitehall Lane, and I was only a street over on Whispering Pines Road. It was a fun neighborhood to grow up in, with a fishing pond and a baseball field and a public library for easy summer reading, all near our homes. Junior was a year younger than Lawless and I and the rest of our working gang. We were to graduate from Albany High School in 1975 where we had played sports together, had grown up together. We gave Junior hell a lot, even when he didn't deserve it.

Junior's parents, Bud and Claire, were from Vermont, were Catholics like my family and had four other boys and a girl. Bud and Claire became friends with my parents, Bill and Joann, and the couples went out to eat and had drinks together. The LaMoys were fun to be with. But Junior was routinely late for our one-day-a-week job. He had trouble getting up, a little more than the rest of us. And we never missed an opportunity to give hell to a brother lint head.

"The *boy LaMoy* ain't never on time," I said.

"Daddy Roy's gonna carry Junior's ass to the gate!" Lawless said, now feeling at least good enough smile.

"Carry ya to the gate!" was a Roy Davis phrase meaning that we were not working hard enough, playing too much, or sleeping on bales of cotton, and Roy was going to escort us to the front of the mill where the security guard was posted and make us leave. We would be fired from the mill. Roy never carried any of us to the gate. He said it frequently, we deserved it a lot, but we never got it.

Leonard "Law" Lawless drove into Junior's driveway in front of his house and Junior came out carrying a grocery sack for a lunch bag. He got into the car, and he looked bad and smelled worse. He had stayed out late too. His hair was matted, and from the inside car light when he opened the door, I could see that his eyes were streaked red. He looked like a lint head ready for work.

"Get in!" I yelled purposely loud. "Get your ass in the car!"

"Easy, Daddy, easy," Junior said. "I got a bad head."

"You've had a bad head all your life," I said. "The hell with your head, Junior, did you brush your teeth? Your breath smells like someone threw a bucket of assholes at you and half of them stuck."

"Yeah, John Boy, I brushed my teeth," Junior said, "but it didn't do no good."

"Junior, next time try usin' toothpaste instead of horse piss," Lawless said as he backed his big blue car out of Junior's driveway. We were headed to the cotton mill.

Daylight was almost breaking, Sunday morning papers had been delivered, and on the streets we passed few cars, turning onto Slappey Boulevard and then onto Eleventh Avenue that would take us to the mill built in the early 1900s. It was quiet on these streets, and the looms would be too.

It was 7:15 and we were 15 minutes late. Daddy Roy and our lint head brothers were waiting at the gate. Roy tried to look angry. There was Donnie "Hatchet Head" Spence, so called because he boastfully reminded us that he could use any tool, drive any vehicle; David "Lover Boy" McClung, who liked telling Roy about his girlfriends and Roy liked listening; Mike "Skinner" Trotter, whose response to most situations was, "Well, boys, I reckon we could skin it back and let the gnats have it." In South Georgia, the gnats have anything they want. And finally, there was Ray "Tubby" Macolly, a little shorter and heavier than his mill-working buddies. Sometimes Roy called Ray "Lard." Other times he was "Lard Ass." If not our specific mill names, we were all referred to as "Daddy."

There had been other Sunday high school lint heads, like Donnie's older brother Ricky, who had worked there, left, and had passed the job on to us. The boys that morning at the gate were my brothers of the mill. Roy was our mill daddy.

As I was getting out of the car with Law and Junior, I saw Junior reach into his grocery bag and grab something. It was something that we had been planning to give to Roy.

"We're gonna give Daddy Roy and Moody a present," Junior said with a grin stretching to Tallahassee. Moody was the mill's Sunday security guard, uniform and all. "Our Daddy will take a snort."

It was a bottle of Mellow Corn liquor. Maybe the closest thing to moonshine sold legally, that's what Roy used to say, but he still preferred real moonshine. I had never tasted Mellow Corn, never would, but I had smelled it the first time we'd given Roy a bottle. It was weeks before my nose and head recovered.

The three of us walked toward the gate where the others were waiting.

"Junior, where ya been?" Roy said.

"John Boy wasn't ready," Junior said trying unsuccessfully to cover his ass.

"Roy, you may need to use your belt on Junior for lying to Daddy," I said.

"Damn your mule-hide Junior, I'm gonna carry ya to the gate!" Roy said as we were all standing at the gate. Roy was trying to act strong and authoritative, adjusting his gray ball cap on top of his head and spitting tobacco juice true, like a Henry Aaron line drive. He wore the same cap to work each Sunday. It looked like he had gotten it when Aaron started playing in the 1950s. Roy kept his shirts tucked in his pants, worn with an old leather belt. He wore work boots, brown and faded. Unless he was eating or drinking, he kept tobacco in his mouth, sometimes Red Man chewing tobacco, sometimes snuff. When he became agitated with us, he spoke quickly, and juice dripped down his chin and onto his shirt and he'd stop giving us hell and say, "Momma ain't gonna like that." Anna, or Momma, washed his shirts for him. Roy almost had a full set of teeth. The ones he had were stained yellow, some even brown. He smiled and laughed anyway.

Then Junior held up the bottle of Mellow Corn as if it had been a relic found in an ancient cave.

"*Tallahassee, Daddy!*" Roy said. "Are you gonna give your daddy a snort? *Tallahassee, Daddy!*"

"Tallahassee" was Roy's word when he spoke excitedly about something and wanted us to be excited too. Mellow Corn got him and Moody excited. Junior gave the bottle to Roy, and he turned the bottle up to the morning heavens, gulped down a few mouthfuls, enough that would've killed anyone of the lint heads. He pulled the bottle away from his lips, wiped his face with the back of his left hand. He looked more than satisfied.

"Roy, that's gonna kill ya dead when you drink it like that," Junior said.

"*Tallahassee, Daddy!* It ain't gonna kilt me dead," Roy said. "I just took a little snort. That's my medicine, Daddy. But don't tell Momma I took a snort. She'd tar my ass up. Momma don't like me takin' my medicine."

He passed the bottle to Moody who drank it exactly as Roy Davis had. Then we went to work.

NINE

Sundays at the mill it was just us, the lint heads, Roy and Moody. Roy's "boss man" would occasionally come into the mill, and when he did, Roy became visibly worried about whether we were actually working or sleeping or playing one of our mill games. Roy was right to be worried.

With the mill quiet and empty on Sundays, we had been hired to clean the weekly accumulation of lint and dirt in the air conditioning and ventilation systems. We were paid minimum wage for eight hours, but it usually took us about four hours to complete our work. That left time for other things.

That morning as we walked through the mill toward our work areas, I was next to Roy, and Leonard Lawless was walking in front of us. Law was wearing a bright red jacket with large lettering on the back. It said FIRESTONE. Lawless' father, John, worked for the tire maker that began production in Albany by the late 1960s. His family had moved here from Iowa. Law's father took us fishing and camping, and my dad would take Lawless and me to the ball field, hitting grounders and flies. It was a good time to be a boy.

Roy saw the back of Lawless' jacket, stopped walking and extended his right arm pointing to the jacket and said, "*Ford!*" He seemed proud of himself believing that he had correctly read the one-word message on the jacket, a little boy wanting the praise of his parents for making the honor roll in school. I said nothing.

Roy was the only adult who could not read or write that I had ever spent considerable time around. At the end of each workday,

Roy would carefully, taking several moments, write his name on time cards indicating who had worked that day. Roy wanted us to see that he could do this thing, make some marks of a world unknown to him. That was the extent of his literacy.

At the mill I once asked Roy about his school days and he said, "I went in one door and out the other."

We walked through the mill that morning over stained floors blackened with tobacco juice and enough cigarette butts to give a smoker cancer. We went around motionless looms by dust-covered walls, and metal carts used to push spools and cotton throughout the mill. Lint was everywhere and in some places so thick it was part of the mill's physical self. In other places, in all other places, there were degrees of coating, maybe some from the 1940s when Roy was a young man. By the end of the day lint covered me whole, ears, nose, head, and entire body. The inside of my nose, by the time I showered at home, would be full of black mystery.

The mill itself was still and silent and the machines, raw and metallic, were of long, long ago.

That day like other Sundays we paired off, teamed up and Roy sent us to different parts of the mill to begin working. He wanted to believe so anyway. Before we departed, we got the signal from Hatchet Head Spence, our leader. Hatchet Head was the first of our group to become one of "Roy's Boys," and later he was able to help the rest of us secure our mill jobs. We owed our lint-head world to Hatchet Head.

When Roy walked away from us toward the front of the mill and left us in the back heading to work, Hatchet Head said two words, Rat Patrol.

I went with Hatchet Head to a warehouse along the railroad tracks at the back of the mill. In the warehouse there were many cotton bales, hundreds of pounds each, stacked 25 feet high. We were supposed to clean the ventilation system in that warehouse along the back walls. Instead we lay down on a pile of soft fabric, far enough from the entrance of the warehouse where we could hear

Roy coming because the many keys attached to his belt jingled with each step. There we slept for about an hour.

"Let's go, Uncle John," Hatchet Head said, rubbing his cotton-mill eyes. "Let's get the other lint heads. It's time, Daddy."

I woke up and said, "Time for the Rat Patrol?"

"Yep, sure is. It's time to go to work," he said.

The other lint heads knew we'd be coming, and some had begun drifting toward the warehouse, always looking and listening for Roy. It was too early in the workday for Roy to be checking on us, usually.

We gathered along the row of warehouses where the cotton was stored and the trains stopped. Weapons were found by all of us. The most common were four-feet long concrete-hard cardboard tubes used for wrapping fabric. They were two-inches wide, perfect for swinging. The hunt was on.

Rats in the cotton mill were more than a foot long, and they were fearless. Small children would be in danger. Of all the lint heads, I was the one most scared. And they gave me hell about it. I didn't like going on patrol.

"Hell, John Boy, we're gonna let you walk point," McClung or Lover Boy said. He smiled and slapped me on the back. He loved slapping his lint head brothers. "I want ya to tear their asses up. Make Daddy Roy proud of you!"

"Thanks. That's exactly what I want," I said, staring at him as he grinned at me. I slipped to the back of the patrol, letting Hatchet Head and Lover Boy take the lead. They enjoyed this shit.

We walked slowly through the warehouses for five minutes before coming to a pile of trash along the loading docks with the railroad tracks directly below. There were pieces of wood, cardboard, trash, and other debris in a pile, 10-feet wide and three-feet high. They circled the pile like primeval shamans under a full moon. I was backing away from these Neanderthal hunters. Weapons were ready, and our grips were tightening.

"Steady, lint heads, steady," Hatchet Head said almost in a whisper. He moved closer than anyone to the pile. Not rushing, respecting the hunt and the hunted.

"Hell, Hatchet Head, just pull the damn boards off!" Tubby said. He had raised his weapon over his head, a medieval executioner following the king's order.

"Not so fast Tubby," Hatchet Head said. "Your Daddy needs to get a little closer. It's all gonna be alright."

Slowly, like surgeons inside a heart, Hatchet Head and Lover Boy pulled, gently pulled, a piece of cardboard from the pile. And then another. They waited. Then they pulled another. I saw Law's eyes grow wide, the same way they did when he crashed into an opponent on the football field. He had been ready.

"Git ready, lint heads. You better git your asses ready!" Lover Boy said. He then removed a piece of rotten plywood, about four by four. The lint heads looked on.

A rat shot out from the pile, past the other lint heads coming directly toward me. It came faster than a greyhound, as big as my cocker spaniel at home. It was thick gray, menacing. I was scared. Before I reacted, there was a loud *Whack!*

A club had come thundering down, and now a rat was flattened and blood was dripping out of its mouth. The rat moved a little, but was whacked again and again. Then it was over.

"I saved your life, John Boy, you sissy," Law said, inspecting his weapon for damage. There was little, just red with blood.

"You damn sure did, Law. It's good being a sissy," I said.

I was able to breathe again.

"*Heerre* they come!" Hatchet Head said.

The rats came boiling out of the pile of debris like Japanese kamikaze planes during World War II. I jumped on top of a cotton bale. The hell, I thought, with killing these animals. Let the rest of the lint heads have it all. They were swinging freely, and as rapidly as they could raise their weapons into the air, clubs were striking hard, killing rodents as they fled the pile. Ten, fifteen, and they kept coming.

"Hit 'em lint heads! Hit 'em!" Lover Boy said as if he were our football coach.

Dead rats were lying on the dock, and blood had splattered onto the tracks below.

Lawless, Big Law on Rat Patrol, was the most fine and flamboyant rat killer among us. He had thick long hair that covered his neck, and with each powerful swing his head jerked and hair flew everywhere, worthy of a sideshow at the county fair. He was a natural rat killer.

"You're dead, you piece of shit!" Law said, hammering another one.

"Go, Law! Go!" Skinner said, having stopped the killing himself to admire the work of one of his brothers. "Damn, boy, you're gonna make Daddy Roy proud."

Safe at the top of a bale, I watched and cheered as the killing continued. After a few minutes, the boys were tired of swinging, and those rats that weren't dead had run away. They counted 11 dead and silently looked at them, respectful of their tenacity. Then we heard the keys jingle.

Roy walked up to the dock where we were and looked down at the dead rats for ten seconds, turned his head toward the railroad tracks and spit tobacco juice six feet down onto the tracks. It landed near a spot of rat blood.

"You kilt a heap of 'em," Roy said. He looked at the rats more than he looked at us. He began counting the rats pointing his right index finger at each one of them and saying the number out loud. He stopped after eight and then stared at us.

"Now *git* to work, you lard asses!" Roy said.

And we did.

TEN

One Sunday we were sitting on top of the mill near large gray metal tanks that were full of lint and needed cleaning. Roy was with us. He reached in his right pants pocket and retrieved a pocket knife that looked too old to open. But it did. He sat down on the concrete slabs that held the tanks and then took his boots and socks off. Each sock had at least two quarter-size holes. With the knife open and in his right hand he grabbed his left foot, bent his knee slightly, and pulled the foot close like a doctor examination.

"Oh Daddy, my pigs are killin' me bad!" Roy said. "My feets hurt terrible."

Roy's toenails were a sickening dark yellow, and they had grown around his toes as if to purposely form the letter *U*. His feet looked as if they had completed a 100-mile death march in two days at the bayonet point of an invading army. But how long would it take for toenails to grow that long? Roy wasn't altogether sure.

"Daddy when's the last time you trimmed those things?" Junior said.

Skinner didn't give his daddy time to answer.

"You need to skin 'em back and let the gnats have 'em! *Tallahassee Daddy,* those things are nasty."

"Skinner, leave Roy alone about his pigs. Why don't you just skin your dick back and let the gnats have it," I said.

"Now, John Boy, I'm sorry if I hurt Daddy's feelings," Skinner said, not sorry for a damn thing.

"Don't you boys fret about my pigs," Roy said. "Momma still loves me."

"Roy, she may love you but your damn toes are gonna rot off and maybe your feet too," Junior said.

"They ain't gonna, Junior," Roy said, spitting tobacco juice toward where Junior was sitting. He didn't hit him though.

Roy carved and trimmed his toenails for ten minutes with his aged pocket knife before he was satisfied. He hacked away inches of toenail, and they did look better. But it didn't change the ugly color of his feet. He put his socks and boots back on, his knife in his pocket and smiled with a stream of juice rolling off his face.

"Roy, I guess you're one hell of a surgeon," I said.

"*Tallahassee,* Daddy! They feel good now," he said. "All you lard asses need to *git* to work. Let's go Daddy, let's go."

We went back to work and swept and cleaned using black water hoses that we sprayed into the gray tanks, pushing heavy lint down drains where rats and snakes live and hide. Later that day the lint heads met in one of the warehouses. We had worked enough.

Hatchet Head picked two teams. The teams separated out of sight from one another to find the long cardboard tubes that we used to kill rats with. This was the only weapon allowed when we warred, not with the rats, but with each other. Besides not aiming for the head or crotch, there were no other rules. The lint heads believed in only a few rules.

After a few minutes of gathering armaments, we met again in another warehouse where there were two yellow forklifts, 200 cotton bales stacked on top of each other, plus an area of open concrete, no-man's land had no protection. Hatchet Head had selected the warehouse, like a general determining advantageous terrain. It would start with a formal declaration.

"You son-of-a-bitches can kiss my ass!"

From the other side came the response.

"We'll kick ya'll's ass! You chicken shit lint heads!"

Now it was on.

Some throws were true while others fell harmlessly on the cold, smooth concrete. We jockeyed for position using forklifts and cotton bales as cover and strategy. And hoping for the right angle, we might surprise a fellow lint head. A lint head can move fast sometimes.

At one point I was behind a forklift crouched like a catcher without his mitt. I had my weapon in my right hand ready for delivering. I was looking for an advantage. Ten yards away were three cotton bales that provided better cover. I waited for a lull in the fighting and then took off.

Running full speed from the forklift to the bales, I believed I had made it safely until I saw Hatchet Head, leader of the other team, who had positioned himself out of sight but near the bales I was heading toward. Oh, shit, I thought. And I was right to think that.

He fired striking me at the base of my back, and I instantly felt a piercing river cut through my backside. I fell to the floor - a dove shot from the sky.

"*Ahh...ahh!*" I said. I couldn't breathe or talk for a minute.

"I got your ass," Hatchet Head said.

"You damn sure did," I said.

He and his team knew I was hurting and fired no more at me. The hit produced a baseball-size black bruise at the base of my back. It hurt badly, and I took myself out of the battle. I drifted off to the far end of the warehouse, away from danger.

I found safety on top of some bales and could clearly see the fighting. My hurt slowed no one but myself. I saw that Lover Boy had outflanked Big Law, who was my comrade during this battle.

"Oh, shit, this doesn't look good for Law," I said, but no one heard me.

Lover Boy hollered a Rebel Yell as if he was serving under Confederate general Stonewall Jackson, and Law turned around to confront him. It was the wrong move for Law. Lover Boy heaved the cardboard tube, violently striking Law an inch below his left eye.

Thick blood began flowing down Law's face. He was dazed and had dropped to his knees. I'd played football with him, and he was as tough and stubborn as anyone I had ever played with. I'd seen him bleed on the football field but not like this. Blood was now covering his shirt, dropping on the warehouse floor, just like blood from dead rats.

"It's over," Hatchet Head said. All lint heads dropped their weapons and encircled Law.

"Shit, man, I'm sorry, I'm sorry, Law," Lover Boy said, bending over Law and looking at that awful thing he had done.

"Get 'em some paper towels," I said.

Lover Boy ran to the bathroom and returned quickly with a wad of brown paper towels pulled from the dispenser. The cut was more than an inch long and into the cheek bone.

"I been hit good Daddy," Law said, reaching for towels from Lover Boy. Blood continued down his face.

"Damn, boy, you should've ducked," Skinner said, of the skin-it-back-and-let-the- gnats-have-it philosophy.

"Yeah, you're right Skinner, I should've seen him sneaking up behind me – you dumb ass," Law said.

After ten minutes sitting on the floor, we got Law to his feet. He could stand on his own, and the bleeding had stopped some from the pressure he had been applying to the cut. But it was still a mess.

"We gotta get him to the hospital," I said.

Law needed eight stitches to close the cut under his eye. His cheek was blue, black, and swollen as if he had taken a full Muhammad Ali punch.

After we got back from the hospital, Roy saw Law and said, "Daddy, this one looks like Bad Eye."

Law had a new mill name. It was perfect for the best rat killer in the mill.

•••••

The rattlesnake was stretched out six feet across the mill floor, its body a beautiful pattern of gray, green, and yellow. It was thick in death having eaten well off mill rats. The snake's head, once large and shaped like a triangle, had been smashed flat. It lay along the same pathway that we took each Sunday morning.

Moody, the security guard whose eyes lit up when he drank Mellow Corn, had used an iron rod to beat the snake to death. He had done a good job of it.

"*Shhh, Shhh,* that's a mean un," Roy said, speaking quietly as if he might awake the dead snake.

Moody had cocked his baseball cap upright on his head, smiled and leaned down two feet from the viper and said, "Not no more."

"He sure would taste good in the skillet," Roy said. "Yes, sir, Momma could fry 'em up good."

The lint heads stared at the snake a few minutes before going to our work stations. Roy took the snake home to Momma.

That morning I was working with Tubby on top of the mill cleaning lint from the gray tanks. It was cold and rainy and the clouds over the mill were moving low and fast like that rattlesnake had once been able to do. All the lint heads had our Sunday bad heads. We had had a keg party the night before.

"John Boy, I'm 'bout to fall out," Tubby said, using a phrase from the exhaustive football practices our coaches demanded.

"Tubby, do what you need to do. I'll cover us for awhile," I said.

"Thanks, man. I gotta lay down," he said.

Tubby looked pitiful. He felt worse. He lay down on the concrete slab with a cold light rain sweeping across him and began sleeping immediately. As I began working, I looked at his motionless body. The boy was tired.

I continued to clean one of the tanks using a water hose and a spray nozzle that wasn't working properly. I tried to tighten the nozzle but couldn't, and water continued dripping from it down my pants and onto my black rubber work boots. But I kept spraying, still able to knock down giant chunks of lint like small trees falling in a silent dark forest. Then Tubby began snoring as if he was a mighty train on a midnight run. He was a peaceful 30 minutes into his first nap.

Maybe, I thought, Roy wouldn't come out in the rain and check on us.

Fifteen minutes later gray clouds started breaking and patches of blue appeared in the distance. I could see clearly from the top of the mill. It was still cool and windy, but sun rays were streaking across the mill. Blue now was everywhere the sky was.

Then I heard Roy's keys. He was coming up the steps that led to the concrete slab where I was working and where Tubby was sleeping.

"Uncle John, that's *good*, Daddy! You workin' *good*," Roy said. Roy did not see Tubby further down the concrete foundation and on the other side.

"Roy it's gonna be alright, but this nozzle isn't workin' too good," I said.

"What's the mule doin', Daddy?" Roy said.

"I don't know what's wrong, Roy. I've been tryin' to tighten it, but I can't," I said.

Roy leaned his head six inches from the nozzle as I continued spraying lint and getting wet myself from the leak. He watched me, intently, spray for two minutes.

"*Heere*, let me see that old girl, Daddy," Roy said.

Roy took the nozzle from me and looked at it as if he was searching for gold in a North Georgia stream. He told me to turn off the water and I did. Roy unscrewed the nozzle from the hose and sat down on the concrete platform with his legs and work boots dangling off the backside of the mill. I sat down next to him. Attached to his belt and his pants pockets were rubber washers, pliers, screws, nuts and bolts, screw drivers, duct tape, and a spare nozzle. There were other tools I couldn't identify, and those were just the things I could see. He was a two-legged toolbox.

He began to work on the nozzle, a well-trained soldier defusing a bomb. His eyes remained focused while his short, brawny fingers and dirty black nails carefully moved around the nozzle. I felt as if I shouldn't say anything during this ritualized inspection, but I did anyway.

"Roy, what's wrong with the damn thing?"

"I don't know, Daddy, but I'm tryin' to fix her," Roy said. "She done quit like a cow's tit out of milk."

Roy turned his head sharply away from me and spit tobacco juice off the side of the mill and re-focused on the nozzle. He wasn't in the mood for talking. But I was.

"Roy, how long have you been workin' here?"

"I was 'bout like you when I started," Roy said, pulling a new rubber washer from his toolbox belt and putting it in his front shirt pocket where he kept two pens and a pencil. He used a screw driver to remove the old washer from the nozzle.

"I bin here since," Roy said, spitting more tobacco juice. "Left once to help my daddy on the farm and then in the service. That's all, Uncle John."

"Why did you work in this place?" I said.

He looked away from the nozzle and into my eyes with his eyes wide now in remembrance of days passed.

"*Shiitt*, Daddy, I had to have food and help my momma," Roy said. "What else a man gonna do? The mill bin good to me and Momma. We always had some food."

Roy told me to bring him the hose, and he re-attached the nozzle to it. Then he told me to turn the water on. The water came out of the nozzle as Roy squeezed and sprayed, harder and truer and without leaking like it had when I was using it. He sprayed for a minute, and still no dripping, he was satisfied and gave the nozzle and hose to me.

"Roy, that's workin' a lot better," I said. "I just didn't know what was wrong with it."

"Don't they teach ya nothin' in school?" Roy said. "Don't they teach ya any kind of learnin'?"

"I guess they don't, Roy."

He turned from me and began walking toward the steps leading down the concrete platform from the top of the mill back into the mill. His keys jingled and his footsteps purposely splashed the pools of rain water, a little boy having some fun. He finally noticed Tubby still sleeping and a little wet. Roy walked over to him, looked down upon him and gently kicked Tubby's legs. Tubby didn't move or wake up.

"If Lard don't git up, I'm gonna carry 'em to the gate," Roy said.

"Roy, I'll get him up. He's not feelin' very well," I said.

"He's gonna feel worse if I carry 'em to the gate," Roy said. "Joe Williams ain't gonna like this half-ass shit."

Roy had evoked the name of one his "boss men," and said it as if he was a feared Roman emperor of the first century. Roy had "boss men" and "big boss men."

"I'll get him up, Roy," I said.

Roy looked down at the sleeping Tubby for 15 seconds and then up at me.

"Okay, Daddy, okay," Roy said. "Be easy with Lard. He needed shut eye. Yep, shut eye good for ya some time, but git 'em up, Daddy."

Roy walked down the steps toward the mill splashing water puddles as he went. I woke Tubby up and let him use the nozzle that Roy had just repaired.

ELEVEN

We were late again to the mill, all the lint heads this time. Roy was waiting for us at the guard house with Moody, both men looking in anticipation toward the parking lot. We had no Mellow Corn on this morning.

Bad Eye came to a sudden stop, gravel flying skyward, in his big blue Ford. Along with Junior, the three of us got out and heard more cars pulling in. The other brothers were behind us. We waited on them before walking through the mill gate, where Roy and Moody were. Daddy Roy's concerns this morning would not be eased by his medicine.

Before we said anything, Roy said, "Joe Williams ain't gonna have no more of this half-ass shit!"

He had been saying exactly that every Sunday lately, and we deserved it. We had become exceptionally half ass.

"We're sorry Roy. We had a short night," I said.

"Sorry ain't gittin' Daddy. I'm goin' give you a *long* day," Roy said.

"Roy, you know we'll get all the work done, Daddy," Junior said.

"Junior, I'm tar'd of your half-ass shit," Roy said, firing tobacco juice two feet from Junior's feet. Roy could kill a man with that if he chose to.

Roy had been protecting us lately from his boss, Joe Williams, who was coming to the mill regularly now on Sundays concerned about our mill games and the diminishing quality of our work. Roy, if he knew, would tell us when he was coming, cover for us the best he could. Williams himself once called the lint heads together and told us "there wasn't going to be anymore of this half-ass shit." He was angry. But it was the half-ass shit that we loved.

That morning Bad Eye tried to ease Roy's worrisome mind.

"Joe Williams is gonna carry all y'all to the *gate*! Ain't that right, Roy?" he said. It didn't help Roy's disposition that morning.

"Bad Eye I'm gonna carry ya to the gate myself," Roy said. "Y'all gonna have Joe Williams chew my ass out one more time – everybody's out the gate!" After that Roy relaxed a little.

We never cared about what Joe Williams might do to us if he caught us sleeping or on Rat Patrol or warring against one another with cardboard weapons. We knew our time in the mill would soon be over, some of us going to college, others finding fulltime work after high school. Until then, there'd be more half-ass shit.

After working for about an hour that morning we took a break sitting on and around a yellow forklift. It was rusted in several spots, its wide black tires smooth from lifting thousands of bales, each one hundreds of pounds of pressed white wrapped in a brown gunny sack held together by metal straps. We had a lot of fun on those bales, sometimes using them as protection during our battles. Other times we slept on top of them. A few times if they were stacked high the way we wanted, we jumped from stack to stack. This scared the shit out of some of the lint heads. And the bales were perfect to hide behind if Roy or Joe Williams were looking for us.

Hatchet Head was sitting in the driver's seat of the forklift. The keys were in the ignition, and he was pontificating on his brilliance in everything he did. This sermon we had heard many times. He told us that there wasn't a vehicle on earth of any size or type that he couldn't drive. That morning he set out to convince us.

His father had bought him a white Monte Carlo, always clean inside and out, but he could drive big trucks, eighteen-wheelers, he boasted. He often drove his father's flatbed truck to Elberton, Georgia, 200 miles away, and back with a heavy load of cemetery monuments used in the family business.

"Anything on wheels, boys," Hatchet Head said. He was as cocky as a Georgia bootlegger on Sunday morning.

"You're full of shit," Lover Boy said.

"Yeah, I am. We're all full of shit," he said.

"I'll bet you a dead rat you can't drive this forklift," I said.

"And I'll bet you a bottle of Roy's Mellow Corn you can't," Bad Eye said. "But you gotta give your *real daddy* a snort if you win."

"I don't want any of that medicine. It'll kill you," Hatchet Head said. "But I will bet you a dead rat."

Hatchet Head turned the key and the forklift began bellowing black smoke and coughing as would a cigarette addict. He pressed the accelerator, and the engine leveled and gained full power. We backed away from the machine giving Hatchet Head the center of the warehouse where the bales were not stacked. He had as much room as a basketball court. I jumped on top of cotton bales to watch.

Now he shifted gears and sped toward the front of the warehouse leading to the loading dock where the cotton comes in. After 30 feet he cut hard to the right, and the machine held true, obeying its new master. Riding high in the saddle, like Roy Rogers in one of Roy Davis' favorite comic books, Hatchet Head was now heading in the opposite direction faster than I thought was possible on a forklift.

"You're gonna hit the water fountain!" I hollered, believing then that our mill days were over.

He was charging bull-like toward the back of the warehouse near a water fountain and rest area for tired millworkers. His grip on the wheel was sturdy as he leaned forward in the black torn-leather driver's seat.

"Why doesn't he smash into the bales instead of the fountain? Roy ain't gonna like this," I thought.

It was part precision driving and lint-head luck that halted the forklift ten inches from the old gray water fountain. He whipped the machine to the left and completed two beautiful circles before stopping. The rest of the lint heads cheered. In the forklift seat, surrounded by stacks of cotton bales, Hatchet Head was the mill god.

"Who wants to take a ride with me?" he said.

No one answered.

"Ah, c'mon you pussies, if you don't ride with me, Roy's gonna carry ya to the gate," Hatchet Head said.

With Hatchet Head remaining in the driver's seat, the rest of us walked slowly toward him and encircled his machine. We were hesitant to get close as if he had driven that yellow forklift down from Mt. Olympus. Gods should be approached cautiously.

"Boys, relax, she won't hurt you," Hatchet Head said.

"Hatchet Head, we won't ride with you on that thing," I said. "Roy doesn't want his lint heads hurt."

"Yeah, I do wanna live to see my baby doll tonight," Lover Boy said.

"I promise I'll go easy. No one will get hurt," Hatchet Head said. "I always take care of my lint head brothers."

Bad Eye walked in front of the forklift inspecting it as if he were back in Iowa at a farm auction. A fearless rat killer shouldn't be afraid of anything.

"Okay, me and John Boy will go," Bad Eye said.

"Wait a minute, Law, I'm *not* gonna ride that thing," I said.

"Now I'm tellin' ya, I'll go easy. Get on, it'll be good for you," Hatchet Head said.

"Good for killin' me," I said.

"Okay, okay, here's the deal. Whenever you want me to stop, just tell me and I will," he said.

"But will you really?" I said.

"Yeah, I will, you know you can trust me," Hatchet Head said.

"Let's go John Boy, don't be chicken shit," Bad Eye said.

"What the hell, I should be chicken shit but I guess I'll go," I said.

I climbed on the forklift to the right of Hatchet Head, and I would be standing during the run while holding to a piece of metal that supported the driver's head covering. Bad Eye got on the other side and was doing the same. The whole time we were securing ourselves, Hatchet Head was moving his foot on and off the accelerator. I got a bad feeling.

"Y'all will be fine, boys, just enjoy the ride," Hatchet Head said.

He drove slowly away from the water fountain as the other lint heads backed away to safety. Hatchet Head was driving slowly. Maybe the spirit of the machine had been tamed. I was beginning to feel better.

"Y'all sure look pretty up there," Skinner said. "You better skin it back and let the gnats have it." He was sitting on top of a bale, his rubber boots tapping the cotton as if he were enjoying his favorite song.

"See, boys, I told y'all this won't be bad," Hatchet Head said. "This old girl is just too tired to put out again."

I was pleased that the girl was tired, and I loosened my grip on the forklift wanting to believe that Hatchet Head was going to play it out like he said. Then he pressed down hard on the accelerator and said, "*Hold on lint heads!*"

My head whipped back hard and Bad Eye's did the same. I squeezed the metal support that I had been holding onto – if not I would've been tossed off the machine and stacked next to the cotton bales. Hatchet Head drove as fast as it would go for 50 feet and then pressed the brakes. The smell of burned rubber and smoke was rising from the warehouse floor and our heads flung again, almost severed from our bodies. He waited five seconds.

Hatchet Head then turned the forklift around and headed in another direction.

"You son-of-a...!" I said, but he didn't hear completely what I had called him. The machine was too loud and my words fractured with fear. It wouldn't have mattered anyway.

He now had us near the center of the warehouse, positioned where our brothers enjoyed full view of this death ride.

"Let's see who can hang on, boys!" Hatchet Head said.

He continued driving in a quick, tight circular pattern trying to throw me and Bad Eye off the forklift. My head was hurting, my vision blurred and all my fingers were aching from the hold I had on the forklift. Soon I would lose my grip and fly through the warehouse and bloody the cotton. I would end up a dead lint head, just like those rats we had killed.

I was about to concede my tragic fate to the cold, cold concrete when Hatchet Head, master of all tools and driving machines, began slowing the forklift. I began to breathe regularly again. He stopped the forklift and turned off the engine. The engine coughed twice and three seconds later coughed again before becoming silent.

"I told you this old girl was too tired to go all the way," Hatchet Head said, smiling all the while.

It took me two minutes before I could see and think clearly.

Bad Eye was dazed, too, and when he came off the forklift, he walked to the nearest cotton bale, lay flat on his back and said, "Don't you hate it when they don't put out."

The forklift ride had left us all exhausted, even those lint heads who had only watched. All of us found comfortable places to sleep on top of cotton bales. We were hidden and scattered throughout the warehouse to be awakened by the sound of Roy's keys.

TWELVE

Roy had come to the top of the mill one summer day after lunch, and when he saw us, we were spraying one another with water hoses. The sweat, lint, and heat had engulfed us all. We needed relief.

Roy sat down next to us, took his boots and socks off, stood up and waded in the water that our hoses had left standing. Sweat was dripping off his face faster than tobacco juice from his mouth. He had been inside working and that day it had been hot enough to suffocate rats and snakes. He looked all worn out.

"Roy, you need a break," I said.

"You're right, Daddy, I do. This here heat is killin' me," he said.

I used one of our hoses to spray his wrinkled and tired feet.

"*Aahh,* that feels good, Daddy," Roy said. "She's hot like a sugar shack today."

"What's a sugar shack, Roy?" Tubby said.

"Lard, you ain't learnin' nothin' in school," Roy said.

"Roy, I don't know what a sugar shack is either," Bad Eye said.

"Outhouse, Daddy! Don't you know nothin'," Roy said.

During the summers when he was a sharecropping boy and even later at the mill village, one of the hottest places in Roy's world was the fly-covered, gnat-coated, rotten-wooded outhouse.

Roy Davis placed his feet into a puddle of cool water, and we sat around him and next to the gray tanks full of lint. The tanks were providing us shade from the sun. Roy talked about growing up on the land in Baker County and hard days in the fields. He kept his feet in the water, and every few minutes I'd spray them again as we talked and laughed a long way from sugar shacks and sharecroppers.

Twenty minutes later he put his socks and boots on, stood up heading back into the mill.

"Okay, Daddy, let's *git* it done," Roy said. "Y'all lard asses need to git with it. Times a burnin' up, and Momma will be here soon to git me. We gotta git the work done, Daddy. I don't want Joe Williams to chew my ass. He's been stingin' my ass like a horsefly on a mule."

"We'll finish it, Roy," I said. "You know were gonna get the job done. We always do."

"*Tallahassee,* Daddy!" he said.

We watched Roy walk away from us. We knew it would be awhile before he would check on us again.

It would be almost three hours before our workday ended, and the sun was pounding hotter around the concrete slabs and metal tanks. Ten minutes after Roy had left, we were still sitting and talking and spraying each other.

"We need a beer run," Hatchet Head said.

"What'd you say?" I said.

"Beer run – let's go to the base," he said.

Donnie Spence's father had been in the military, and the family had access to the commissary at the marine base in Albany. There the beer was cheaper than it was in local liquor stores, which were closed on Sundays.

"Yeah, we can go after work," I said. "Cold beer sounds good."

"No, let's go now," he said. The lint heads initially questioned our leader's decision of leaving the mill without permission during work. Quickly though we conceded to the plan. We always followed his lead, and those cold beers would taste good on this miserably hot day.

It was decided that I would go with Hatchet Head as the other lint heads began pulling money out of their pockets. We collected about 10 dollars before Hatchet Head and I contributed.

"Here, Hatchet Head," Tubby said, handing his lint-head leader 28 cents. "Buy me a case."

"Sure, Tubby, that'll get you two cases," Hatchet Head said.

The lint heads watched for Roy and Moody the security guard, while Hatchet Head and I climbed down the mill on a metal pipe that extended from where we were to the ground below. It was a slow climb with our knees scraping the red bricks and our sweaty hands gripping onto the 30-feet-long pipe.

Hatchet Head had gone first, and once he was five feet from the ground, he released the pipe, hitting the ground and maintaining his balance. I did the same right after him. We both ran hard to his Monte Carlo parked under some tall pines in the gravel parking lot. Driving out of the parking lot, we looked back at our brothers on top of the mill where they had raised brooms over their heads and clinched their fists, pumping them in the air.

"*Go, Daddy, go! Go, Daddy, go!*" They cheered as they saw us in the car heading toward the Flint River and to the marine base.

"Man I told you we'd be alright, John Boy," Hatchet Head said. "No need to worry."

"I never doubted it," I said. But I had, and we still had to get back into the mill without Roy or Joe Williams catching us.

We drove across town to the base, bought a case-and-a-half of 12-ounce Schlitz and drove back to the mill in less than an hour. The lint heads saw us pull into the parking lot. Hatchet Head parked in the same spot he had left, we got out of the car with two brown paper bags full of cold beer and carried them next to the metal pipe that we had used for our getaway. The plan was working. Now, how to get the beers inside the mill?

The plan was simple.

"Catch'em boys! Catch'em!" I said, holding a beer in my right hand before tossing it up to the top of the mill. All 36 would go up that way. I had never seen, not on the baseball or football fields, my brothers so sure handed. They missed not one.

After each can had been caught, Hatchet Head and I ran to the back of the mill and climbed over a chain link fence, rode the elevator to the top of the mill and re-joined the lint heads. Neither

Roy nor Moody or even Joe Williams had seen us. It was a well executed plan. We had been lucky.

The boys had put most of the beers inside one of the gray tanks, and they were floating in the cool water while we each drank one.

"Dang just look at those little boats," Lover Boy said, sticking his head inside the tank.

"Makes you want to join the navy," I said.

"Damn sure does."

Then we heard the keys, and Roy was on top the mill and heading toward us.

"Our daddy's on the way," Junior said, taking another drink of the Schlitz.

"What in the hell are we gonna do now?" Skinner said, looking at Roy but hiding his beer behind his back.

"I don't know, boys. This doesn't look good," I said. "What are we gonna do, Hatchet Head?"

Hatchet Head looked inside the tank at the floating beer, proud of what we had been able to do, and then at us. He hesitated for a moment and said, "We can't do anything now. Roy's here – it's over."

The keys got louder as Roy got closer, and he walked up the concrete steps reaching the platform and then over to the beer-filled tank that we were supposed to be cleaning. He looked inside then back at us.

"How's it look, Roy?" I said.

"We did our best," Hatchet Head said.

Roy pulled his head out of the tank, eyes forever wide. Holy hell's coming now, I thought.

"Damn ya lard asses! I told ya Joe Williams has been chewin' my ass! Now look what you've gone and done now," Roy said spitting tobacco lethally. "I'm carryin' every lard ass to the gate. I don't want Joe Williams to see this."

Hatchet Head used a broom and reached into the tank, pulled one of the beers to him and lifted it out of the water. He said nothing, popped the top of the beer can, readying it to drink, and gave it to Roy. Roy said nothing.

Roy took the beer, turned it up and drank half of it, and then he took out a red handkerchief and wiped across his mouth. He still said nothing. Then he turned the can up again and finished it. He threw the empty beer can back inside the tank with the other boats that were full.

"Git 'em out of thar and git back to work," Roy said. And then he was gone.

THIRTEEN

Our last year at the mill was 1976. The previous September I had enrolled at Albany Junior College, but that fall I would be transferring to Georgia Southwestern College in Americus with Hatchet Head and a few other Albany boys. In June 1976 we planned a high school graduation party for Junior LaMoy at my house. My parents had gone out of town. We invited Roy to the party and he accepted. Bad Eye and I went to Roy's house that night to pick him up. Momma said goodbye to Roy, standing and waving on the front porch.

Roy was sharply dressed in burgundy slacks, a two-inch thick white belt, and a yellow button-down, short-sleeve shirt with a bag of pipe tobacco in his front pocket. That night Roy smoked a pipe. He wore a leather-strapped watch and he didn't have his cap on. His grayish hair was cropped close, still a full head. We drank keg beer, laughed until it became painful, and got our picture taken with Roy. The party was mostly lint heads, current and past, and a few girls did come by.

"*Ohhh, Tallahassee,* I like this beer machine!" Roy said. "It's God-Almighty good. Tastes like honey dew. Makes me wanna honeycomb."

Roy used the phrase "like a honeycomb" when describing sexual intercourse. When he became excited telling dirty jokes, he would lift his right arm high at the punch line and weave his arm and hand from side to side, and whistle at the end, evoking the sweetness of sexual entry. Then he said, "*I likes that, Daddy!*" Or sometimes he said repeatedly, "*Tallahassee, Daddy! Tallahassee, Daddy!*"

Roy never travelled much outside of Albany once he returned from the service after World War II. But I did ask him if he had ever been to Tallahassee. He said yes and that he recalled having some fun there. That night at Junior's party, he was having some fun with us.

"Roy, that beer's good but it's not 100-proof like Mellow Corn," Junior said, wearing a wide-collared plaid shirt and kneeling next to Roy, who was sitting in a lawn chair.

We were under my carport on Whispering Pines Road and had taped a large white banner inside it congratulating Junior for completing high school. We had written lots of messages for Junior recognizing his achievement. Most of what we wrote our parents and young children shouldn't have read. We read some of them to Roy and after each one he said, "*Tallahassee!*"

"This here beer's sweet like sugar candy my momma used to give me," Roy said.

"Sweet like me?" Junior said.

"Junior, you 'bout as sweet as the ass-end of a dead goat," Roy said.

"Now, Roy be nice to Junior tonight. He's out of high school now," I said.

"He's gonna be out of the mill if he don't stop his half-ass shit," Roy said, filling his cup once more from the keg. "Joe Williams is watchin' Junior."

"Roy, you know I work harder than your other lint heads," Junior said, smiling as he put his left arm around Roy's shoulders. "I'm gonna be a boss man one day at the mill and chew everybody's ass out."

"Yeah, Daddy, you 'bout the worse one I got," Roy said, smiling back at Junior.

At the mill Junior was sometimes a one-man freak show. He could flip his eyelids up over his eyes and make himself appear as a creature from a Japanese horror movie. He could suck in his stomach until he looked grotesque. And he could stretch his arms behind his back to the extent that they caused his shoulder blades to protrude like lethal projectiles. Taken whole, these acts could've been top billing at a travelling circus. I never knew another boy who could do all these things. Roy sometimes saw Junior's performances at the mill and it amazed him.

"Junior done made himself ugly again," Roy said following each exhibition.

"That Junior is something special, ain't he, Roy?" I said.

"Yep, 'bout like two goats fuckin' in a pile of cow shit," Roy said.

At the party that night a couple of times Junior would look at Roy and say, "This is for you." Then he flipped his eyelids up until you could see the pink underneath them and left them that way for 30 seconds.

Around midnight we drove Roy home from the party, home to Momma. Bad Eye drove, and I rode up front with him. Junior and Hatchet Head were in the back of the LTD with Roy. He had been talking about Momma and she had left the front porch light on for him. We pulled up in Roy's driveway on Sixteenth Avenue.

"I gotta go see Momma now," Roy said, getting out of the car.

"Roy, we'll see you at the mill," I said.

Roy was now standing next to the car but turned around and looked in the backseat at Junior.

"Make sure this ugly one's on time," Roy said.

"I'll be on time, Daddy," Junior said.

I got out of the car and walked Roy to his front door and returned to the car. We drove past the cotton mill on the way to my house. The party was over and Roy was with Momma.

•••••

A few weeks after Junior's party, we were back at work on top of the mill and being reminded by Roy that Joe Williams was keeping a hot trail to the mill, more and more agitated about our activities. Roy kept telling us that Joe Williams had been watching us. That Sunday afternoon, clear and hot, I was watching something else.

From the top of the mill, I could see nearby Satterfield Baseball Park where I had played on high school and American Legion teams. For several minutes I watched the game that was being played. I had missed baseball that summer, too old to play for the legion and Albany Junior College did not field a team. I was planning to play the following year at Georgia Southwestern College in Americus. I had missed the smell of leather and green grass freshly cut and white-lined diamonds of red dirt. And I had missed being with a team and playing that "simple, beautiful game," as my father said of the game that he taught me when I was a boy in Indiana.

Roy had played baseball when he was in the navy and stationed in Virginia. He had been a catcher, the same position my father had played on a semi-professional team before we moved to Georgia in 1966. It's the most demanding position, and the catcher is the only player who can fully see his eight teammates. A catcher calls pitches for his pitcher working in harmony and providing leadership to his battery mate. He must withstand the pounding of foul balls, pitches that hit the dirt and then hit him, and base runners willing to crush him in order to safely reach home. A catcher needs a strong and accurate arm, and be able to become a steel wall of determination. I bet Roy was a good catcher.

"What ya doin', Uncle John," Roy said, having walked from the mill all the way to where I was standing without my hearing his keys. I had been concentrating on the game, adrift in another time and other places.

"I'm workin' hard, Roy."

"Okay, okay, that's *nice.*"

Roy looked away from the mill toward the baseball game. The midday sun was making it difficult to see, and he put his right hand, as if saluting, in front of the bill of his cap to block the sun. He could see better now.

"I loved playin' ball," Roy said, steadying his hand, eyes looking ahead, memories of his navy-playing days surfacing during that afternoon at the mill.

There was a foul ball hit deep behind the catcher who had first misjudged it and lost his footing but recovered to make the catch. It was a fine play.

"That thar was a good un," Roy said.

"Yeah, nice catch," I said.

We watched the game together for about 10 minutes and said little to one another. Finally, Roy turned to go back inside the mill.

"Well, gotta git back, Daddy. You git ta work like the rest of 'em," Roy said. "Don't be a lard ass."

"Okay, Roy. I'll get back to work now."

I watched Roy walk back into the mill and began spraying the lint again with the water hose. I sprayed for a few minutes and quit. It was too hot to breathe. Hatchet Head and Lover Boy were on their way to see me, and they weren't interested in working either.

"John Boy, we need to cool off today," Lover Boy said.

I aimed the hose at him, sprayed him fully from the neck down and filled up his rubber boots until they overflowed. Then I turned the hose on Hatchet Head.

"Is that what you wanted?"

"Hell no," Lover Boy said.

"We're goin' swimmin' and I don't want to hear any of your shit about why we shouldn't," Hatchet Head said.

"You boys are too big to jump in the tank with the lint," I said.

"No, man, we're goin' to Shoreham," Hatchet Head said.

Shoreham was an apartment complex where we had attended swimming parties, and it was a few blocks from my house on Whispering Pines Road. This was a day for swimming, with this sticky heat, but I felt uneasy about this adventure. Joe Williams was lurking in my thoughts and maybe in the mill itself. But I could tell by looking at Hatchet Head and Lover Boy that it would be useless to argue this one. The decision had been made. We found the other lint heads, and no one objected.

We rode the dirty, lint-covered elevator down and walked through large rooms where looms sat silently in this awful heat. We looked for but didn't see Roy as we walked to the back of the mill along railroad tracks to a chain linked fence that we climbed over. From there we came around to the front of the mill where our cars were parked. We saw neither Roy nor Moody.

Having made it to the front of the mill, Hatchet Head said, "Run, boys! Run! It's a getaway!"

In the gravel parking lot, Lover Boy ran past Junior and accidentally bumped into his right shoulder and Junior fell to the ground. Lover Boy stopped to help him up, but he slipped and fell too. Two-feet-tall rubber boots are not conducive for running.

As I was running, I stopped and saw the pile of rubber boots tangled together, like two turtles that had flipped over on their backs unable to move. It was a great scene, but there was no time to enjoy it.

"Git your *ass* off of me!" Junior said.

"I'm tryin' damn it. I was tryin' to help your sorry ass," Lover Boy said.

"Let's go both of you before Roy sees us," I said.

I reached down and grabbed Junior's right hand and helped him onto his feet. Lover Boy got himself up and the three of us began running again toward where the getaway cars were parked. We agreed on Bad Eye's truck.

Lint heads jumped into the back of a black Ford pickup truck belonging to Bad Eye's father. The truck often had a camper attached to its bed but not that day. I was riding in the front as Bad Eye sped out of the parking lot, leaving dust and gravel behind. Once on the paved roads away from the mill, he slowed down and hot air blew over the lint heads in the back with hair, sweat, and lint everywhere.

"Go Bad Eye go! Go Bad Eye go!" came the chants from the bed of the truck. I could hear the cheers over the sound of the engine and the wind it had created.

We drove easy now through neighborhood streets with few cars, tall live oaks that shaded the streets near the mill, and across

Slappey Boulevard, where teenagers cruised during weekends, and then on to Shoreham Apartments. Bad Eye stopped at a stop sign, and I looked through the truck window to my mill brothers in the back. The wind had matted their heads still dirty with cotton lint, and they had taken their shirts off but still had on dirty pants and black rubber work boots. They looked like mill boys who could've been working when Roy was a young man. These lint heads had a lot more fun.

When Bad Eye stopped in the parking lot by the pool, there were only a few people swimming. We got out of the truck, walked to the pool and jumped in. That was it. This was what we needed. Even though the water was warm from days of 100-degree sun, it was good to be in it. We floated, swam, and fought one another in the water, working harder wrestling than we had at the mill. After 30 minutes we decided to leave.

"We better get back. Roy's probably looking for us," I said.

"Shoot, John Boy, our Daddy won't know we left," Lover Boy said.

"Sooner or later he will," Hatchet Head said, stepping out of the pool.

Wet but cleaner now, we got back into the black truck and Bad Eye drove us to the mill. We needed to finish our work. Back at the mill, the parking lot was quiet, no sign of Roy at the security office. We didn't see Moody either. It looked safe enough to walk through the main entrance. Roy was probably looking for us at our favorite sleeping spots in the warehouses. We walked past Moody's office. It's all going to be okay, I thought as we headed for a door that led into the mill itself.

"We made it, boys," Skinner said.

"Damn sure did," Tubby said.

I reached out to open a door that would take us back to work.

"Boys, where y'all *bin?*"

It was a clear, angry, high-pitched voice. And it wasn't Roy's. Joe Williams, the "boss man," was directly behind us and Roy was behind him. Roy had the frightened look of a child who knows he's about to be harshly disciplined by his father for some horrible misbehavior. All the lint heads were worried too. My hand was still on the door knob, but I didn't open it. We all turned around from where the voice had come.

Joe Williams and Roy had been waiting on us hidden from view in the security office, a long way from the swimming pool. Now we were had.

"I asked you boys, where y'all bin?" Williams said. His face was red with explosive powers.

"Mr. Williams, uh…we, uh, uh…we went swimming," Hatchet Head said.

I could see Roy's lips tighten and his eyebrows contracted, but he didn't say anything. Roy was as tight as a snuff can that he couldn't open. Williams looked at each of us and back at Roy and repeated it.

"I told you boys that I was damn tired of your half-ass shit, and I meant it," Williams said.

"Yes, sir, Mr. Williams," Hatchet Head said. "We shouldn't have left the mill. That was the wrong thing to do. We're sorry and it won't happen again."

"Mr. Williams, we apologize. We won't ever do this again," I said.

But this was not working.

"No, son, I guess you won't." Williams' face had contorted even further. He looked like he wanted to hit us.

"No, sir, we won't ever mess up like this again," Hatchet Head said. "We all realize that we've made a mistake and we need our jobs. This will never happen again."

Hatchet Head was convincing and maybe Joe Williams would give us one more lint-head chance.

"No, son, you *realize* this," Williams said. "Today is your last day in the mill. You boys will never work here again. All of you can turn around, walk through that gate, and go home. I told you I was tired of your half-ass shit – it's over."

He opened the door that led into the mill and walked through it and around the dirty looms. There was nothing Roy Davis could do to help us.

"Well, boys, it looks like our lint-head days *are* over," Hatchet Head said, no longer in his apologetic tone. He expressed more cockiness than remorse.

Roy looked both frustrated and disappointed, knowing that we wouldn't be working with him anymore. We had had some good times together.

"Daddy, I told y'all that he was-a-watchin' us. Daddy, I told you," Roy said.

"Roy, you were right. We just screwed up too many times," I said. "We're gonna miss you, Daddy."

"Okay, Daddy, okay," Roy said, patting me on the back.

After our last day at the mill, we saw Roy a few times that summer, stopping at his house with some cold beer, and one time we brought a bottle of Mellow Corn, his medicine. That fall of 1976, some of us went off to college, while other lint heads married and began work fulltime. Roy Davis retired from the mill a few years after Joe Williams had fired us.

FOURTEEN

The next time I would see Roy Davis would be 25 years after I had left the mill. The lint heads stayed close over the years. We were college roommates, groomsmen in our weddings, and our children became friends with one another. Our close friendships that had begun in elementary school have remained that way into our 50s and will, I'm certain, until the end. When we're together, we often talked about "Daddy Roy" and our lint-head days. The more I thought about Roy over the years and our days at the mill, I decided that I wanted to learn more about his early life, and write his story.

Someone had mistakenly told me then, and I do not remember who it was, that they thought Roy had died. Late in 2001 when I telephoned his home on Sixteenth Avenue, I expected Anna or one of his children or maybe a grandchild to answer the phone.

But the voice on the phone sounded like Roy Davis.

"Is this Roy Davis?" I said after I heard a cracked "hello."

"Yep, this here's Roy Davis. Yes, sir, it's me."

"Roy, this is Bill Lightle. I used to work for you at the mill. You called me Uncle John."

"Were ya the tall one, Daddy?"

"Yeah, Roy, I was taller than the rest of them."

"Did ya live on Stuart?"

Roy was referring to Stuart Avenue in Albany near Whispering Pines Road where I had actually lived.

"No, Roy, I lived on Whispering Pines. You came to my house once for a party."

"Okay, Daddy, I 'member ya," Roy said.

•••••

It was the second time in a few weeks that I had driven Roy to his boyhood home in Baker County, where he grew up picking cotton bound for the mill. I wanted to see where his family had been buried. The winter sky was low and gray, but there were stretches of blue that were becoming visible and out of sight again. I drove over red-dirt roads by fields green with winter grass that cows were eating with their heads extended to the earth.

"Just a little ways more," Roy said. "Right up thar and we'll stop."

I pulled into the driveway of Traveler's Rest Cemetery at Free Will Baptist Church. The church was a small building next to a ranch-style, red-brick house, and they were the only two buildings near the cemetery. Behind the cemetery was a pine forest, and in front were many acres of pasture land where cows were grazing and black birds, small ones and big crows, were flying over the field, some stopping to peck the land.

A chain link fence enclosed the small cemetery that was guarded by a cluster of large live oak trees with Spanish moss. I came to a stop under one of the trees, and we got out of my car and walked through a gate that led to where his people were buried.

Roy was losing his eyesight and because of that I thought that I would have to read other grave markers before finding those of his family. He took only a few steps through the cemetery gate using his smooth walking cane and stopped. Roy stood in that spot for a minute, and I was directly behind him. I looked beyond Roy at the white and gray tombstones, and further still to the cattle in the fields.

"I think they're back yonder," Roy said, lifting his cane steady with his right hand and pointing it to the back of the graveyard.

After taking five more steps Roy was walking a bit steadier now, confident he was headed in the right direction. I remained behind him, slowing my walk to read tombstones along the way. Roy stopped near one of the gravesites.

"That thar's my grandma," Roy said. "She's the one who took care of me."

The marker simply read: Lizza Davis, 1852 to 1945.

She had been born nine years before the war that ended slavery and died the same year another war ended after a dictator slaughtered millions while attempting to enslave Europe. It was the tenderness of his grandmother on this land that mattered to Roy, love and care remembered by a sharecropping boy unable to read about history's meanness.

Roy looked away from his grandmother's grave and showed me others.

"That thar's Daddy's brother."

Charlie, 1895 to 1972, had fought in World War I. He was a PVT CO "D" 51 Infantry, the marker said.

"Roy, do you remember where he was during the war? Was he fighting in Europe?

"No. I don't 'member whare it was."

One of Roy's brothers, Hubert Davis, Sr., 1924 to 1993, was buried there. He had been a master electrician and World War II army veteran.

We continued and found where Primus Davis, Roy's bullwhip-swinging father, was buried. He was born December 20, 1884, and died one day after his eighty-first birthday. Next to his grave was a plot reserved for his second wife with a marker in place: Myrtle I. Davis, October 22, 1914. Myrtle had been born two years before Roy's birth. She was that young girl who Primus "ran off with," leaving his first wife Ollie, Roy and other children. I telephoned Myrtle Davis, who was still living in Baker County then, but she didn't want to talk about her life with Primus.

"Do you ever talk to Myrtle?"

"Nope, not for a long time ago. I must've said somethin' she didn't like. I don't know 'bout it. No, sir, I don't," Roy said.

We saw other family graves before leaving the cemetery.

"Where's your plot?"

"Me and Momma got ours at Riverside."

Riverside Cemetery is in Albany near the Flint River which weaves through Southwest Georgia on the way to Lake Seminole, in the Southwest corner of the state. It once provided a market route for cotton, picked with slave and sharecropping hands.

Roy's only surviving brother was Glenn Davis who lived in Texas but had been confined to a wheelchair for several years following an automobile accident.

"He don't have no legs. An eighteen-wheeler ran over him. He was in a Volkswagen," Roy said.

We got back in my car and drove out of the parking lot past fields and cows and over dirt roads before coming to a smooth paved road. After ten minutes, I turned onto Georgia Highway 91, which would take us back to Albany. The clouds that had covered us earlier were moving faster now, freeing endless blue skies. I asked about his mother, Ollie.

She had been buried in Florida where she was living before her death, and along the ride Roy talked more about the life that he had lived, a life made rich by a woman forever devoted to him. He spoke of the hard life and of the hard liquor he sometimes drank.

"I never did drink anything under a 100-proof," Roy said, as if issuing an official proclamation.

The Mellow Corn that the lint heads and I had given him was the closest taste to moonshine, a taste he first knew as a little boy. During that ride I thought about what his daughter Bobbi Buffi had said, "That daddy would've been an alcoholic if not for Momma." She said that Momma always "stayed on him" about his drinking.

"You still drink, Roy?"

"Nope, I stopped a few years back. Momma never did like me takin' a snort."

Momma's strength and love have sustained Roy. Undying, unyielding, a forever-in-the-earth-and-sky love, it's the thing that makes this life worth living. She had the children and disciplined them, worked on the land and in the home, made the business arrangements to buy their own land, and she searched for scrap lumber, found some and helped Roy build their home. She hauled, sweated, and lifted even after becoming pregnant and sick with child. She worked alongside Roy, building something better than they once had. When her children's marriages and relationships failed, they came home to live with their daddy and momma, bringing grand-children, too.

"All my chil'en bin married twice," Roy said. "But Timmy's bin married three times."

Roy and Momma, that frail mill-village angel, were married in 1938. All those years of struggle and love with the country and world endlessly changing, Roy and Momma did not.

"How'd you and Momma stay married all these years?"

"I'd let her be tha boss for awhile and I'd be tha boss for awhile."

"Is that what it was, Roy?"

"Yep, Daddy, that's all."

Roy's eyes were beginning to water inside and were showing red. His words and memories were stirring the emotions of an old man coming to the end of one love-filled life on the way to another. I wanted him to talk more about Anna and what she had meant to him. But he didn't say anything else about her. He didn't have to. Roy never used a lot of useless words. He had something more than words were able to convey - Momma.

"Whatever happened to Moody, the security guard?"

"Moody died not long after y'all graduated from the mill."

"How long did he work there?"

"Long time, Daddy. Thar ain't many left that worked with me."

"Roy you spent a long time in that mill."

"I had to work mighty hard. They got the best part of my life, but I enjoyed every minute."

It was a struggle for Roy to do the simple, beautiful things in his life. Both Roy and Anna have had heart surgery. A nurse regu-larly visited their house to bathe him, check his blood pressure and to ensure that he's taking the prescribed medication. His eyesight continued to worsen. There were big pecan trees in his yard, and in the fall, for many years, Roy walked the yard gathering pecans. Now, because he can't see them, he lay on the ground stretching out his arms and legs to feel for them. Anna had recently injured her hip helping Roy pick up pecans and had to be taken to a doctor for treatment.

"I felt so sorry for Roy," Anna said a few days before my trip with Roy to the Baker County cemetery. "He can't see. He takes his foot and feels for the pecans. If I would've stopped when my hip started hurtin', I'd bin awright. But I wanted to help 'em."

During that cemetery trip Roy said, "Daddy, it's awful when you can't see nothin'."

"Roy, you got us to the Baker County cemetery. You did fine."

"I did okay, Daddy."

"You did great."

"I got to git back and check on Momma," Roy said. "I think thar's somethin' I need to do for her."

The afternoon sky was clear as we passed the Albany Airport and turned left on Slappey Boulevard and then onto Sixteenth Avenue where Roy and Anna lived, around the corner from the Flint River Textile Mill and the old mill village.

I was taking Roy Davis home to Momma.

EPILOGUE

A few months after my interviews with Roy and Anna Davis, she suffered a stroke and required full-time care. Her family admitted her to Palmyra Nursing Home in Albany, just around the corner from the old mill village where she had met Roy in the 1930s.

With Momma gone, Roy moved into his son Leroy's home outside of Albany.

"Leroy would drop Daddy off at the senior citizen center on Pine Avenue, and they had a bus that'd take him to the nursing home," Bobbi Buffi said. "He'd spend all day there. Him and Momma would have lunch and dinner together."

I spoke with Bobbi in early 2009 at her beauty salon on Third Avenue where she said that some years ago Roy was involved in a car wreck not far from Bobbi's shop. No one was hurt in the accident, and Roy walked into her salon after it had happened.

"He was a little hyper when he came in," she said.

He walked around the shop for a few minutes, described the wreck to Bobbi and finally said, "Well, I best call Momma and see if she's awright."

Momma wasn't in the wreck. In Roy's mind, since that day in the village when he first saw his angel, Momma was wherever he was, even if she wasn't there.

"They were very devoted to one another. They were inseparable," Bobbi said.

June Morris has worked with Bobbi for 15 years and got to know well Roy and Anna.

"He liked women and he had an art and a gift of making every female feel special. Both of them were so extra special," June said.

As their bodies deteriorated the past few years, they received help from family members, nurses who came into their home, and from Habitat for Humanity Inc., the worldwide organization that builds homes for the impoverished. Habitat, some years ago, painted, repaired, and fixed leaks in the Big House that sits next to the Pink House. But bodies are harder to fix.

In 2005 Roy was diagnosed with prostate cancer and was hospitalized. During this same period he had suffered a stroke.

"Daddy went downhill fast. He had gone totally blind by then," Bobbi said.

Doctors, according to Bobbi, had said Roy was too old to operate on, and after about two weeks in the hospital, he was gone.

On October 19, 2005, Roy Davis' hard-working and hard-loving body and soul passed from this world to another. Roy is buried at Riverside Cemetery along the Flint River, near the heart of Albany.

Next to Roy is Anna's plot.

In this world and the next, his angel remains forever close.

•••••

LaVergne, TN USA
29 October 2009
162427LV00002B/4/P